TALES of a SOD HOUSE

Stories of the
Kansas Frontier
as told by my mother,
Helen McCauley Merkle

Baby

D1531237

Ellen Verell

Back Cover: Illustration by Sherry Cunningham, depicts the sod house as it would have looked in 1898.

International Standard Book Number: 978-1-60643-245-7

Library of Congress Control Number: 2008911899

Cover design by Jim L. Friesen

Printed in the U.S.A by Mennonite Press, Inc., Newton, Kansas

Dedicated to the memory of my parents,
William J. and Helen McCauley Merkle,
Both of whom were Children
Of early settlers on
The Western Kansas Prairie.

TALES OF A SOD HOUSE BABY

Stories of the Kansas frontier as told by my mother,
Helen McCauley Merkle

An only child, Helen McCauley, was born in the sod house built by her parents on their homestead site, ten miles northwest of the present town of Fowler, Kansas. She didn't begin to recount her earliest years until well into her eighties. Fortunately, her long-term memory was still indelibly sharp and she loved to laugh and reminisce about how she looked at the adult world around her, mostly family, when she was still in her formative years. I write it mostly in the first person because that is how she told it to me.

She liked to recall that she had lived from the horse and buggy age, through the jet age and had seen photos of a moon landing. She read everything she could on world affairs, politics, government, health and social issues up until her eyesight failed her completely. She remembered Theodore Roosevelt as the first president her parents mentioned and she was his life-long fan. However, the subject nearest and dearest to her was "family" and re-telling the stories of her parents, aunts, uncles and cousins as well as some of her close friends always brought a certain light to her eyes. She genuinely enjoyed the stories of "early days."

By her ninetieth year, she remarked to me, "I must be one of the last living sod-house babies left in this county!" I could not be sure but I think she may have been right. Her birthday was October 15, 1899, a year that saw the last of the sod houses built new. The twentieth century ushered in more prosperous-looking frame construction with plenty of gables and "gingerbread" trim. Sod houses marked the end of the homestead era. The following are my mother's tales as nearly as I can reconstruct them.

Ellen Verell

TABLE OF CONTENTS

1-DESTINATION: WESTERN KANSAS

Among all the things that would be different in my life if I had not been the child of early settlers—almost everything would have been! I wouldn't have learned to like head cheese, blood pudding, or aged beef, for example—a real treat for the pioneer family. I wouldn't have known the comfort of eating corn-meal mush sweetened by sorghum molasses on a cold winter night, because it was available when other food in the house was less plentiful.

No outings to pick plums and wild grapes, no wild rides to herd cattle, no picnics in the neighbor's enchanted grove, no midnight rides with my adoring aunts and cousins. I will never know how different I might have been if I had been allowed to finish high school and perhaps graduate from some eastern college, pursuing a profession or career that would have led who-knows-where.

All I know is that I'm thankful I had such good parents and caring family. I realized early on that I was truly blest by the family ties I had inherited. I could look about and see that I had received much in my pioneer heritage that some could only dream of. Those who shaped my life were of strong character and courage. Life on the prairie didn't deal kindly with cowards or the weak-willed! However good or bad I turned out, no one could deny that I had plenty of good examples to follow! Although not faultless, most of the Tullises and McCauley's I knew were God-fearing , enduring people full of the Puritan Ethic—the kind that made good pioneers in the settling of the West.

Charles and Eva Tullis came to Kansas from Iowa in 1887, leaving behind a nice home and some degree of prosperity. Their respective families, the McCabe's and Tullises, had stood with the Union Army during the war with the Confederacy. Great-grandfather Charles Tullis rode as a Captain with an Iowa regiment.

It was apparently my grandfather's desire to brave new frontiers. Grandma was a real homebody who doted on family and friends. He said that their doctor had told Grandma that she needed to live in a drier climate because she was in danger of getting "consumption." This probably played a part in his seeking out new frontiers in such a dry place!

My mother was seven-year-old *Jessie Luella Tullis*, the oldest of three Tullis children who made the journey. She recalled many times in her adult years how she had heard her mother sobbing into her pillow every night during and after the wagon trip that brought them to Hamilton County, Kansas, to a point south of what is now Coolidge. The town still has a small degree of its early day fame because it is marked as the "jumping off" place where the Santa Fe Trail took a more southwesterly direction toward Santa Fe, New Mexico.

"Grandad's" full name was Charles W. Tullis. My grandmother always called him Charles. He called her Evie, as in "evening," important because her twin called Eva, as in "ever," was spelled the same! They were daughters from a colonial era Vermont family named McCabe. Charles and Evie, also called Eve or sometimes Eva, decided as early as 1886 that they would seek their fortune in Kansas.

Grandad headed west from Lee County, Iowa, with his good friend, Len Hubbard, who shared the "frontiersman view" of settling new lands. Each man filed a homestead claim in Hamilton County and built a dugout home to house the Tullis family on their arrival. They returned to Iowa full of enthusiasm for the proposed sale of their homes and the return trip to Kansas.

My mother, Jessie, was born February 22, 1879, so would have been about seven, going on eight, at that time. Her brother, Wiley, was about 18 months younger and my Aunt Edna was two years younger than Wiley. They were pretty excited at the thought of a long journey in a real wagon and had no concept of how many days and nights it would take to reach their destination. My mother did recall many times how her mother didn't share the childish enthusiasm that infected her children. Regardless of her distaste for hot sun, dust and smelly animals, Grandma boarded the wagon and pretended to be as cheerful as was humanly possible. Len Hubbard and his wife, Lizzie, had no family at that time, so they were helpful to my Grandma in looking after the little Tullis brood. When the going got rough, Grandma would sing hymns to the children. By the time they got to the western border of Kansas, the children had a good knowledge of all their mother's hymns! It helped them in later years when their lives were full of stress.

After several minor adventures along the trail, the family was thankful to arrive in good health, without any major accident enroute. The family settled into the sod dugout in one day and soon after that, Grandad and Len headed for Len's homestead, nine miles down the Arkansas River bottom to the south. Nine miles is quite a distance by horseback or wagon. Why they chose to be so far apart, no one knew, except them. Each man must have had his own vision of what he wanted his ranch to be. Maybe they planned on owning all the nine sections of land between them! They took a sod cutter to cut out uniform pieces of sod for the walls. Sod was just the native grass held together by its own roots. Len wanted his house above ground, not a hole-in-the-ground, so it took a lot more "doing" to get it built. They left early one day, right after morning chores were done, and intended to put in a full day of backbreaking work in order to get all four walls up—a tall order for one day!

They had not had time to get to the Hubbard homestead when a really bad snowstorm came up. The wind howled and swirling snow made visibility near zero. Grandad's milk cow was in an open-front shed built of driftwood gathered from the river. Grandma realized the snow would swirl around it and cover it completely in a very short time. To keep the cow from smothering in the snow, Grandma decided to go out to free her from her stall. She tied a rope to the doorknob so that she could find her way back to the dugout.

She said later that she would not have made it back to the dugout without the rope to guide her. In the night a herd of horses belonging to a neighbor six miles away, ran right over the top of the dugout. Grandma could just see those horses breaking through the roof and coming in on top of her family but that didn't happen. In the night, however, a dog found the dugout and came down the steps to the door, whining to be let in. Grandma had been warned about stray dogs and the dangers of rabies on the prairie so she did not let him in. Mixing a stray dog in with her three young children was something she couldn't bear to do, even if the dog froze.

Grandad came home the next day, worried that Eve and the children might have been buried in the snow. He was relieved that they had not only been safe but that Grandma had managed to save the cow! He went immediately to look for the cow and found her alive but needing feed. That very afternoon Grandad's neighbor to the west came looking for his dog. He was joyful to see the dog alive, with only a slight frostbite on one ear. Surely the stairwell to the dugout had saved the dog's life because it had been terribly cold in the night. Both dog and master shared their joy at being reunited and Grandad said he was terribly happy to find everyone in good condition.

He and Len had really had a close call in the storm because the blizzard struck them about a mile from Len's homestead site. They would have gone past the site without seeing it, for the storm was so thick and white, except for the fact that they stumbled upon a pile of sod that Jessie and Wiley had built up while playing over there a few days before when they had gone with their dad to "help Uncle Len" even though some of their childish help was questionable. That pile of sod enabled Grandad and Len to find the home site and get into the little bit of shelter available. It turned out to be enough to save their lives and kept them from being frostbitten.

Three bachelors arrived in the vicinity and staked their claims to homesteads near the Tullis and Hubbard claims. They built little sod shacks. Having no families to care for, they came over and helped Grandad—a lucky break for him! They helped him dig his well and build an aboveground sod house and barn. At least one of them worked for Grandad most of the time. They built the house over the door of the stairway to the dugout so that the house had a storm cellar under it and a nice storeroom. The house was almost a mansion compared to the dugout! It had two bedrooms, a big kitchen and pantry and a big living room. The kitchen had a big bay window. They finished the inside walls with plaster. That made it almost rodent-proof. Burrowing rodents were always a problem for sod houses! The roof was covered with boards, then tarpaper, and then sod. It was leak-proof after it settled and the tar- paper kept the dirt from sifting down between the boards. The sod house was much cooler in summer and warmer in winter than a frame house would have been because the walls were about two feet thick. The window made a wonderful spot for the little children to play in the winter when bad weather kept them inside.

The well proved to be a good one, with good-tasting water and plenty of it. Being so near the river, it never went dry, even in the very driest times. Grandad built a long, shallow tank for the water to run through so that they could cool the milk they stored in large stone jars. From that shallow tank, the water was piped down to the corral where the cows had a tank to drink from. Grandad said it was wise to put your well close to the house because it provided cold water to drink and cows didn't care if their water was cold or not!

The sod house built around the well and its tank was called "the well house," and later was called "the milk house" because that was where they stored all the milk. Grandma would skim all the cream off the milk because it rose to the top surface and could be easily skimmed with a big spoon. She saved the cream until she had enough to churn with the dasher churn—a stone jar with a wooden dasher in the center. The kids like to churn the cream and would take turns at moving the dasher up and down. They liked the "splashing" sound and could tell when the butter was beginning to form. It made a different sound as the butterfat formed into solids and the "buttermilk" became more like water.

Grandma "worked" all the butter with a curved wooden paddle until she got all the buttermilk out of it that she possibly could. She saved all the buttermilk for cooking and drinking. She put the butter into wood "prints" that held about one pound, made just for that purpose. She wrapped it in damp cloths and kept it in a stone jar to keep cool. When it was time for Grandad to go to Syracuse again for supplies, she would put a damp quilt over the jar and send it sixteen miles to be sold to the grocer.

Town dwellers were tradesmen and merchants who relied on farmers for their produce and dairy products, then as now. Some of the homes in town had a pitcher-pump over a hand-dug well but many did not. Those who did not carried their water from a neighboring well. Gardens in town were not even an option, for every drop of water would have had to be carried in a pail!

One night when Grandad was in town, he had a bad misfortune. He usually stayed overnight because he always had a load of something to bring home. A round trip in one day would have been very tiring for both him and the horses. He stabled his horses in a livery barn so they would be safe. About 11 p.m. there was a cry of "fire." A fire could be terrible in those days because there was no plentiful supply of water anywhere and the town wells had no "water pressure" as cities today have. The men who discovered the blaze were able to get out only a few horses and Grandad's two best mares were not among those saved. Worse still, the dog had followed Grandad to town and he had tied her up inside the livery stable so that she wouldn't get lost! He said he could hear her cries even above the cries of the horses and that nightmare haunted him for a long time.

He would wake up in the night thinking that he could hear the horses and his beloved dog crying for help that he couldn't bring. The man that pitched hay down for the horses had been smoking a pipe and everyone thought he must have started the fire accidentally.

Grandad recalled this incident to me many years later, after I was grown. He emphasized to me that bad things could always happen, no matter how much we might try to take every precaution to prevent or avoid them. He said that blaming himself for the sad fate of his horses and dog was simply a fruitless exercise. He couldn't go back and un-do the thing that had sealed their fate. He couldn't keep on blaming himself. He had to let go and move on.

The important lesson, he said, was to use good judgement the next time so that history wouldn't repeat itself. If a man could learn from a lesson, all was not lost. If he couldn't learn from it, then he would make the same mistakes over and over. Ever after that, he was extremely careful about inspecting a stable before he left his animals there in the care of others!

2- PRAIRIE STORMS AND OTHER HAZARDS

Storms were a big part of life on the Kansas prairie. One day when it had been unusually still and hot, my grandparents noticed big, dark clouds forming that were almost purple. They were afraid it would be something terrible so took the little ones to the dugout beneath the house. The roar of the storm sounded so loud that they were almost sure it would be a tornado. It passed about a quarter-mile away and proved to be a devastating hail storm that beat a trail about a mile wide and five miles long, hitting two houses, smashing window panes and pounding holes that went through the wooden roofs. They said the hailstones were larger than hen eggs and left destruction that looked as if the ground had been plowed. Not a blade of anything was left standing where it had ripped through the county. They felt very fortunate to have been left out of that storm! Hail storms proved to be a way of life in the summer time; they lost crops more than once but were blest never to have their house struck by one with large hailstones.

The three bachelors got discouraged. None of them stayed to prove up their claims. Other people with children moved in and the need for a school became apparent. Grandad Tullis and some other fathers of children gathered to build a sod schoolhouse near the center of the area where most people lived. It was about three miles from most of their homes. One man, a newcomer, lived very close to the school site. He had a huge dog chained up at his house.

The dog strained and pulled at his chain all the time to get loose. The men had the walls of sod about five feet high by noon and were going to eat a picnic dinner prepared by their wives. My Uncle

Wiley and Elmer, the young son of the newcomer, were sent over to Elmer's house to get some milk for the coffee. When they approached, they saw that huge dog lunge at his chain and break loose. They ran as fast as they could to the school site where most of the people were inside the sod walls. There came the dog, frothing at the mouth and acting completely crazy. He ran in among the horses that were tied to the wagons but didn't bother them. Grandpa had a greyhound tied to his wagon. She was afraid and tried to get away. Grandpa went to his wagon and got his gun to shoot the attacker but just as he pointed the gun, the dog lunged for him and hit the barrel of the gun. Grandad and the mad dog rolled over together while the dog was snapping and biting the gun barrel! The dog heard the greyhound, Fanny, whining in fear; so he dropped the gun barrel and attacked Fanny, grabbing her by the jaw and tearing her face horribly. He just hung on while she cried out in pain. Finally one of the men got his gun and shot them both with the attacker still gripping Fannie's face in his teeth.

After it was all over, the owner of the dog said that he had been afraid his dog might have been bitten by a rabid dog that had been killed awhile before they came there; but he wasn't sure. Since he thought so much of his dog, he didn't want to kill him until he was sure. That was why he had been keeping him chained. His dog had fought with some of the neighboring dogs a day or two before the man decided to keep him on the chain. He had been running loose among many dogs in the neighborhood! It meant that nearly every man there had to kill his dogs or run the risk of having them go rabid and bite a human being. Grandpa had to kill his other two dogs just to be on the safe side! People were so mad at the owner of the dog that he thought it best to leave. They moved away quietly one day and no one ever saw them again. Ten scholars were left to attend classes!

An older sister of one of the pupils taught the term. There was only a three-month term in those days. The school was the life center for everyone, the "hub" of social and religious life. It was used for a church, *literaries*, social gatherings and any other get-together of the community. A generation later, came *Chautaquas*.

The settlers really proved the adage about man's being a "social animal." As soon as a food supply and housing could be provided, settlers began building a meeting place big enough for the neighborhood to convene in one group!

Book learning was important but so was socializing. After all, that was how the younger generation would be able to meet someone from another family! Among people with any education at all, one could not look for a mate among his own immediate family. The Bible was clear on that point and most people had read enough of the Bible to understand that marriage must be between un-related families or at least very distant relatives, such as fifth cousins. To marry a close relative was taboo, even on the frontier.

Glossary of terms, Chapters 1-2

Aged beef-*beef hung in a tree in ambient temperature of 40 degrees or less. Steaks and roasts were cut off, as needed and were exceptionally tender.*

Blood pudding-*The blood of the butchered animal was baked with chunks of bread or biscuit dough or cooked slowly in an iron pot until thick and "pudding consistency." Seasoned with salt, pepper and sage.*

Chautauqua-*A program of re-enactment of famous persons' speeches and orations as interpreted by the actors of the day. Patterned after the Chautauqua, N.Y., summer mission schools and reading circles.*

Corn meal mush-*Fresh ground corn meal, mixed in cold water first, was added to salted, boiling water and cooked to a thick mush. Served with salt, pepper, butter, molasses or even milk, it made a tasty gruel.*

Cold mush could be fried and served with molasses, like pancakes.

Head cheese- *The head of the slaughtered animal was cooked several hours in a large, iron pot. The contents were scooped out and mixed together with salt, pepper and other seasonings. Cooled, this made a thick spread for bread or biscuits. This is still served in many countries, as are liver, tongue, sweetbreads, heart and kidney.*

History time line-*Grover Cleveland was President in 1888.*

Homestead Act of 1862-*Under Abraham Lincoln, Congress passed this act to allow a quarter section of land, 160 acres, free to settlers who would build a home and live in it five consecutive years. This was an incentive for people to move into the West. By 1890, the entire western frontier had been claimed.*

Literaries- *programs held usually monthly at schools for recitation of literary works, poems, speeches, plays. These were a large part of community life on the frontier. Combined with "pie suppers" they were a successful social event.*

Section *–Measurement one mile square, equal to 640 acres.*

Quarter Section-*Measurement ½ mile square, equal to 160 acres.*

3- WILD HORSES OF THE PRAIRIE

One story both my mother and her sister, my Aunt Edna, told me was about a black stallion that ran wild on the prairie. He used to steal mares from the ranchers' herds whenever he could. He stole so many mares that the ranchers got together and decided to make a drive on the wild herd. They got most of their mares back in the drive. The wild stallion lost so many mares, either caught or run off, that he had only a few left.

One morning when Grandad went outside he saw a wild mare with a newborn filly on the hill. He got Grandma, Jessie and Wiley to get on their horses to surround her and bring her into the corral. She wouldn't leave her little baby. Since it couldn't travel very fast, she was easy to drive into the corral. Later Grandad broke the mare to ride. Grandad always carried a little extra grain when he went into a pasture to catch a horse to ride for rounding up the herd. He carried a little pan on his saddle for feeding the grain. The filly began to follow him around, nibbling the grain at every chance. She grew up to be quite tame and never offered to pitch when they saddled her to ride. They named her Nellie and she became a favorite of all the children in the family. Her mother, the wild mare, never did become very tame. She would jump and begin to buck if she got frightened or if she saw a rabbit jump up beside her or if anything happened to startle her.

Grandad gave Nellie to Aunt Edna and she loved her all of the mare's nineteen years of life. She was a pretty, chestnut sorrel. All of her seven colts grew up to be gentle, reliable saddle horses. The black stallion was another story. He hung around and would come in with the other horses to drink at the tank if no one was in sight. Grandad would shut the gate after the horses had drunk and wouldn't open it again for two or three days. He filled a barrel about half full of water and put a rope with a slip noose around the top of it and tied the other end to a post he had set for that purpose. The post had a big signboard in front of it and Grandad hid behind that and held the rope. The horse was so thirsty that he came right in when he saw the gate open and no one in sight. He would come in, stop and snort and then run out. After he had done that a few times, he came to the barrel and put his head in a little way but still snorted and acted frightened. After about an hour of doing this, he put his nose to the water to drink.

Grandad jerked the rope and it went around his neck. That stallion ran and squealed and reared and pulled until he choked himself down. Then the man that was helping Grandad put a halter on him and a rope without a slip noose, running the rope down through the ring of the halter and then another rope the same way. They tied the ropes to two posts that had been set for their big catch; then they let the stallion up. As he ran, they took up the slack until they had him between the two posts. Then they stretched the ropes tight and thought they had him. They didn't know just how wild he was. He jumped straight up and came down on his head. They couldn't stop him. He just kept doing it until he broke his neck. That was the end of the black stallion. There was no more mare-stealing after that.

4- RUNAWAYS, AN UNFORESEEN HAZARD

Butchering meat was a big task and hard work. It was a very important work because people had to have food for their families. Meat could be stored in the winter cold just wrapped in a sheet and hung from a tree or a tall post. It could also be salted and stored in the cellar in jars of brine. But it had to be butchered first. Since it was such hard work, neighbors often helped each other. One day Grandad and a neighbor were butchering some hogs. They had already killed and dressed three big ones and had hung them up on a pole that was laid across two poles set in the ground to support the weight. The children were at school during the day. No one thought of what would happen when they came home.

Old Beauty, a mare who was usually very gentle, smelled the blood and then saw all those hogs hanging up in mid-air. She became frightened—so frightened that my mother, Jessie, the oldest, couldn't hold her. Beauty made a jump to one side and caught Jessie between her body and the cart shaft, leaping into a dead run, with poor Jessie hanging onto her and being carried along. Grandad got on a horse and went after her, expecting to see her all mangled by the horse's hooves; but she managed to hold onto the mare's mane and kept her feet up away from those pounding hooves. Aside from having a very sore side the next day, where the cart shaft had held her to the horse's body, she was all right and had no bad injury—learning about runaways at a tender age! My mother, Jessie, became a skilled rider at a very young age. She almost "lived" in the saddle until she got big enough to drive a horse pulling a plow. Then she "graduated" to plowing while Edna and Wiley did the herding.

Back to butchering: people had to butcher their meat in those days when they had cool nights because they had to be sure the animal's body heat was all out before they could salt the meat down to cure it. Grandma trimmed all the fat off and rendered it, packing the lard in big crocks or jars to keep until it was all used for cooking. All the cooking and baking was done with lard or beef tallow—usually lard. It was considered a very fine shortening and it made wonderful piecrusts! No one knew anything about any kind of "fat" except animal fat. It was hard for an animal to put much fat on his bones out on the open range. Country people worked from dawn to dusk so they didn't have a problem accumulating fat on their bodies, either!

In winter, a quarter of beef or fresh pork could be hung up from a wire between two posts. Covered with a sheet to keep it clean and free of flies, it would form a thick crust on the outside and stay good until it was consumed. The steaks and roasts were delicious and very tender. This could only be done in the winter when the temperature didn't go above forty degrees in the daytime. Sometimes when the nights were very cold, the meat would freeze and, if well wrapped, would hardly thaw in the daytime.

5-RANCHER VS. FARMER ON THE FRONTIER

The cattleman-versus-the-farmer was not just a fictitious theme for western movies made in the 20's and 30's. There was quite a bit of friction between the groups in the 1880's. It was farmers who brought barbed wire, also known as "barbwire," to the west. Up to the late 1870's, fencing with wire was unheard of in the West.

Hamilton County had two big ranches, the Tufel ranch up the river from Grandad, and the Collier ranch to the south. Everyone liked the Tufel cowboys and their foreman but the Collier ranch had a bunch of rowdies who came into town shooting and yelling and always looking for a fight. Grandad said the manager of the livery stable was frightened every time they came to town because, when they saw him, they would shoot right over his head and he was afraid that someday they might not miss him. So he kept out of their sight if he could. It was all free range then without fences to separate one man's land from another's. Grandad had a nice herd of cows and horses. Everything he owned had his brand. He was able to grow all the feed he needed for winter and the grass was abundant for summer grazing. The big ranchers did more or less decide what went on at roundup time and herds would get mixed together at times. That was just unavoidable.

Grandad had a very large water tank that would hold enough water for his livestock for a week. It was pumped full by a windmill. Western Kansas was always quite windy so he never had to worry about water for his livestock. His stock didn't go very far away as they came home for water and their grass was plentiful. When big rains would come and fill the draws and the buffalo wallows, sometimes the bigger holes would hold water for three or four weeks. Then the cattle would wander farther because they didn't have to come home to drink from the tank. That meant Grandad and the kids would have to go hunt them and bring them back closer to home. The big ranches' cattle would wander away from the river and just keep going until their water supplies dried up. If they were a long way from the river, they could get very thirsty. Some of their cowboys would come looking for them but sometimes not soon enough.

Mr. Tufel and some of his cowboys used to stay all night at Grandad's while looking for their cattle. They would sometimes take my mother, Jessie, and her sister and brother for rides on their horses. That was a wonderful experience for adventuresome kids!

Grandad had a five-foot high barbwire corral around his water tank and kept the gate shut after his stock watered and went back out to eat grass. That kept stray cattle from coming in to drink all the water. One time, when a big rain had filled all the holes and draws with water, the big ranch herds had gone way past their water supply and had become too thirsty when the supply ran out. They were almost crazy for water. Grandad and his family were in bed for the night when they heard an awful noise, almost like thunder. It was a big herd of Collier cattle stampeding for the water tank. They had smelled it! When they came to the wire fence around the tank area, they pushed right on through it. The ones behind just kept pushing and trampling those in front. They smashed the water tank and pushed through the fence on the other side. They just kept on going toward the river. Grandad said a stampede is a terrible thing to see because the injured ones can't get out of the way and the cattle from the back of the herd just run right over everything and everyone in the way. He had to rebuild his corrals and his water tank. Rebuilding is never as exciting as building something new because the anticipation of the finished product is not there! Having to rebuild what nature or other hazards could destroy was an ever-present possibility on the frontier. Hiring people to "rebuild" anything was just not an option. Necessity was indeed the mother of invention and the settlers honed their inventive skills repeatedly! This inventiveness through necessity became known as "American ingenuity." People on the frontier were pushed to the limits of their inventiveness and, quite often to the limits of their endurance.

Glossary of terms, Chapters 3-6

Buffalo wallows- *small, shallow water holes also known as playa lakes.*

Settlers- *those people who went into raw, unsettled land to make their living off that land, to establish rule of law, civil government, schools, churches and cultural institutions. The term "Settler" is distinguishable from "immigrant" in that the latter goes into a land already settled with people who have established the government and institutions pertaining to civilization. Settlers come first. Then immigrants.*

Steam Thresher- *machine for harvesting grain, invented by Cyrus McCormick, 1834, not mass produced until after 1884.Not used in western Kansas until the very early 1900's.*

6- TEDIOUS WORK, SOWING AND HARVESTING

The kids would drop the seed on the ground and Grandad would go over the planted ground with a harrow to cover the seeds. A harrow had little iron "teeth" in it that bit into the ground only very slightly. The kids loved planting time because they got to do something that was a real help to Grandad. They took pride in doing it right, too.

Another grain Grandad planted was Jerusalem corn; the stalk didn't have much flavor but the grain was sweeter than milo or cane. It grew about three feet tall and the top made an elbow turn, with the head growing right on top, hanging straight down from the stem. The grain was white with a little black spot on the side. Each grain was almost round, just slightly flat and larger than milo or cane seed. Grandad used to gather some heads while they were still soft. He would rub it and hit it on the wash board to hull it. Then Grandma would cook it for hominy. Sometimes she would use slightly salted water and they would eat it with sugar and cream on it, as a cereal. Everyone liked it. The chickens and pigs liked it a lot better than any of the other grains. Cows would fight over it to get a whole head at once.

Grandad would have my mother, Jessie, and my Uncle Wiley, cut the fodder with a knife made for the purpose of cutting corn. It was called a "corn knife" and was very sharp. The kids were still pretty small but they could handle a corn knife with great accuracy! The cut stalks, also called fodder, were put into shocks, with a lot of labor involved, of course. It was tedious and tiring to build the cone-shaped shocks. Fodder was the part the cattle would survive on during the cold winter. It was not at all nutritious—just filling for the stomach! The children were really too small for the backbreaking work of making shocks and wondered aloud why the cows couldn't just find them in the fields. Grandad decided there must be a better way so he made a small sled with a sharp knife fastened on one side. He could sit on the sled as the horse pulled it along the cornrow. The knife would cut the corn and he would gather it into his arms and put it into bunches—or shocks. Later, he decided it would be more efficient to extend a knife from both sides of the sled so that he could cut the fodder twice as fast! He didn't cut the Jerusalem corn as fodder because nothing liked the stalk. It had all the sugar in the head and none in the stalk beneath. So he let that fodder stand in the field where it would catch snow in the winter.

Grandad and two of his neighbors went together and bought a sorghum mill to get the juice out of the cane. He built a couple of flat vats and put the juice into the vats. Then they would build a fire under the vats and boil the juice down until it was "just right"—a sticky, sweet molasses. It took a lot of boiling and skimming but when it was finished, it was wonderful sorghum molasses! He would put it in a barrel and store it in the cellar. A barrel would sometimes last two years. Lots of the neighboring farmers hauled their sorghum cane to the mill and made molasses. The mill was run by a horse and fed by hand—very slow work but worth the time. The reward was sweet all through the year!

Grandad bought a header and made a couple of barges for it, cutting his small grains that way. The local farmers came and helped him harvest his grain and they would then go through the community harvesting for all the other farmers. One of the men was a much better "stacker" than the rest, so he did the stacking for all of them and Grandad did the cutting. It took four horses to pull the header because of its great weight. They would put the grain heads on the ground in a circle and the kids would ride horses around to tramp the grain out, with each rider leading another horse. It took some skill because the horse had to keep moving and was never allowed to put his head down to sample the grain. After the grain was taken from the circle, the chickens could eat what was left behind; so none of the grain was wasted. He didn't say how they did the wheat and small grains but I think at that time they were using flails—the same kind that are mentioned in the Bible. A flail was a large wood handle with a smooth "club" fastened to it with a leather thong. Someone pretty strong had to wield the flail because it was much like swinging a baseball bat. You had to be accurate at what you hit. The grain was knocked out of the head that way and then the chaff was separated off as the grain was poured over a screen. Separating the wheat from the chaff was very tedious work. Sometimes the women did it if the men were still in the fields. Neither of my grandparents talked much about getting the wheat out of the heads but I know they did it by hand. At that time, they didn't have the steam thresher this far west. Cyrus McCormick had made it but it was too expensive. Grain was all separated by hand, except that which was "stomped" by horses. Life on the prairie was full of risks—even for the chickens! Chicken hawks seemed to be everywhere and were very good at diving down and selecting a chicken for lunch. Coyotes also would prey upon chickens but they liked young, newborn calves, too. Most of the farmers learned to keep two or three greyhounds. When the coyotes got too bad, the farmers would hunt them down with hounds. Grandad became an excellent coyote hunter because he was a good horseman and a good rifleman.

He and his horse were "one" when he rode; he could fire his rifle from all his best saddle horses. Flinching or shying horses were worthless as hunting horses. So too, were injured horses!

An example, 1895- Jessie told about her brother Wiley, and Cousin Wesley, who visited the family in Gray County. The two boys, about twelve, remained at home one afternoon when Grandad and his brother-in-law went into Ensign with horses and wagon for supplies. The cousins wondered what would happen if they tied two horses together and ran them at top speed in opposite directions. Maybe it was true scientific curiosity or maybe it was the kind of idleness referred to as "the devil's workshop," but they actually tied Grandad's two best hunting horses together with a new lariat rope secured to the saddle horn on each horse. They applied a sudden stimulus with a whip and startling noise, causing the horses to run in opposite directions, throwing themselves to the ground with a hard fall. It took weeks for the horses' strained muscles to recover! Grandad said he had a rope for each one of their bare behinds if needed. They understood the message.

7- NOSTALGIA, A PRAIRIE DISEASE

Some relatives came out to Hamilton County to visit in March, 1892. It was terribly windy and they didn't like the wind or really anything about Kansas. They talked so much about home that Grandma got very homesick for the east. Grandad thought maybe if they moved closer to town, she would be better satisfied.

After living on the homestead five years, Grandad bought a place closer to town, securing his title requirements for the first place. The new farm had a frame house with a big kitchen and dining room combined, big living room and two nice, big bedrooms.

The kids went to school in a frame schoolhouse that had ten pupils; but they didn't feel as comfortable with the new pupils as they had with their old school chums. Five of the pupils were from one family and they had five more of the same family at home. The kids felt as if they didn't "belong." So they wanted to move back to their old school; but of course, they couldn't. A very nice teacher came out from Syracuse on the stagecoach on Monday morning, very early. She would go back by stage on Friday evening around eight. The stage passed about a quarter-mile from the Tullis house. There was a "rise" –or a high spot in the land—about two miles before the place where the teacher would board the stage. The kids learned to look for the light on the stage as it topped the rise; then the teacher would leave the house about that time and arrive in time to board the stage...

In truth, Grandma didn't like the new place any better than the old homestead. Grandad decided they should sell out and move to

Arkansas where some friends had gone—the "land of plenty." It was a big move! They sold everything they didn't want to take. They loaded the rest into covered wagons. The livestock was to be cared for by Len Hubbard until the family could get settled and come back after them.

I always thought Grandad truly adored Grandma because he would do anything to make her happy. He wanted to preserve her health at all costs and he wanted her to have the best environment possible. He had made a terrible miscalculation in going to such an unfriendly climate as Hamilton County! He was willing to do anything possible to rectify that error! Even in their later years together, he did everything he could to give Grandma the best life possible. They were "two flesh become one." So they bade Hamilton County farewell and embarked on a new search.

8- EXODUS FROM HAMILTON COUNTY

Grandad built an extremely large wagon bed on one of the wagons. It was wide enough for grown-ups to sleep crosswise and long enough so they could have a cook-stove in one end. Grandma could cook in it and actually baked bread in it along the trail if they camped overnight. The children's job was to gather enough dry cow chips to keep the fire going in the stove! It was a challenging job. Finding cow chips dry enough to burn was not easy! The beds folded up during the daytime so there was enough room to eat inside the wagon. There were five children by that time, so fixing food on the trail was not an easy job.

Another couple was going east so they traveled with the Tullis family. Grandad had four horses to a wagon and one spare, plus his saddle horse—fourteen in all. The other family, Dasher's, had two horses so it took a lot of feed and grain just for the trip. Grandad bought the feed and grain from farmers along the way. Most of them were wonderful about selling him corn; only once did he find a man who wouldn't sell any corn to them, even though the man's bins were full to the top...

They camped the first night near the river, just twelve miles from the farm—one mile below Syracuse. While it wasn't exciting for the parents, the children were so excited that they could hardly sleep! Most of the time they were blest with good weather and they camped in towns near a livery stable where they could stable the horses if there was room. If no room was available, they tied the horses to the wagons behind the stable and brought the feed to them. The two greyhounds were making the trip with the family. In one town, Old Blue was nowhere to be found in the morning. A man told Grandad that he had seen a boy leading a greyhound late the night before but didn't know where he lived. So Old Blue had to be left behind...

Along the way, many sights fascinated the children, who had never been more than fifteen miles from home in their entire lives. One such sight was a six-foot-high fence along one side of the road. Behind it was a herd of buffalo in a big pasture. Some of them came right up to the fence to look at the caravan. It was the first live buffalo the children had ever seen and they loved it! Trains were exciting too, but in a different way! The horses had never seen a train. When the road came anywhere close to the rail track, the horses would become frightened and the adults would have to get to their heads to calm them. The children loved it when the train passed them but the horses never got used to the sight and the noise of a train! Sometimes the trail was so narrow that four horses abreast could not even pass through together. Then Grandad would have to hitch one team ahead of the other to take them through. He would put them back together into the four-abreast pattern because it made the load much easier if they could all pull together equally.

There was an abundance of grass through most of the countryside so Grandad would hobble a couple of the horses and let the rest run loose at night so they could eat. Next morning he would use Old Bob, our riding pony, to round up the horses when they went too far away. The idea was to keep them within sight and sound so that they wouldn't be a temptation to anyone to steal them or a temptation to cougars or coyotes.

Old Bob was a snow-white pony, probably with a little Arabian blood in him. He was completely gentle and the kids loved him. One day, Jessie and Wiley, just for fun, decide to make Old Bob into a spotted pony. They took a can of Grandad's stove black, which was mostly graphite, very fine and very black, and mixed it with some axle grease from the wagon axle. They put black spots all over Old Bob and rubbed them in, even on his legs. He was a magnificent spotted pony! They rubbed until the grease all went in or came off on an old cloth and only the black remained. They washed him with water at one crossing but the spots stayed on. When they went through a town or a camp in town, people would stop and look at the beautiful spotted pony. A man in one town came over to look at Old Bob, ran his hand over him and talked to Grandad about the spotted pony. He asked Grandad how much he would sell him for. Grandad, knowing the spots were temporary, said he wasn't for sale. The man then offered him a hundred dollars for the pony. Old Bob was only worth thirty-five or forty dollars at most. Grandad told the man "You don't want him; the spots aren't real." The man felt some of the spots and said "You can't fool me. I know spots when I see them." Then Grandad told him how the kids had made the spots just for something to do! The man told Grandad "You're more honest than I would have been! I would sure have given you a hundred dollars for him!"

They passed by several empty houses along the way where people had abandoned their homes. Twice they camped beside the houses. The doors were unlocked and most of the windows were broken, so the kids had a big adventure "exploring" the interiors of the houses. One house had two stories and was quite large. It was a real adventure for the kids.

One Saturday morning, the caravan passed near to some relative of the Dasher's. They stopped for a visit while the Tullis family went on to Grandad's uncle's place in the evening. They had quite a reunion. The uncle had a big barn with lots of feed and his corn bins were full of corn. He had a lot of cattle and in one corral he had a bunch he was fattening to sell. He gave them mostly just pure corn to eat and they never got tired of eating—never seemed to get enough!

On the fourth day of the visit at the uncle's house, the Dasher's caught up so the entire caravan started on its way again. Everyone was rested and refreshed and felt good about the journey ahead.

9- THE INDIAN NATION

One Saturday night soon after that, they camped in a grove on the edge of the Indian Territory—now called Oklahoma. Some people called it the Indian Nation. On Sunday, the Indians gathered in the grove in wagons and on horseback, holding some kind of a celebration. They ran races, wrestled, ran horse races and all kinds of competitions. The men and children like to watch but Grandma and Mrs. Dasher declined. They were nervous and wished we hadn't camped there. Two of the Indian horses were tied to one of their wagons eating their grain when they began to fight and kick at each other. An Indian man who was close by chopping wood, threw his axe at one of the horses, burying the axe in the fleshy part of its hip. The handle stood straight up and the horse squealed and kicked but couldn't dislodge the axe. Grandma and Mrs. Dasher were so frightened that they began crying and begging the men to turn around and go back to their homes. The men promised they would turn back to Hamilton County in the morning and they did just that. But the rest of that afternoon they looked around and saw a man who had a lot of hogs—all of them sick or dying with cholera. It was a terrible sight. One of Grandad's mares, Old Beauty, had a baby colt in the night. It couldn't make the trip, being too young to keep up, so Grandad gave it to a man who wanted it. .He had promised the women not to spend another day there! Old Beauty seemed to grieve for a couple of days over her lost colt but then seemed to recover. She and one of Dasher's mules would follow the wagons without being led. They stopped to graze awhile and then would trot to catch up with the wagons. They did this for many days and had always caught up. But one evening they stopped to camp by a stream and, on looking for them, found no Old Beauty and no mule! No one could remember when he had last seen the two.

10- LOST HORSES, LOST CHILD

Since Aunt Edna wasn't much help around camp anyway, Grandpa selected her for the task of getting on Old Bob and going to look for the lost pair. She kept going and going until it finally was getting dark. She came to a green field and there they were! She got around them and started them down the road at a trot. Then they came to a fence with an open gate and turned into that field! Aunt Edna couldn't stop them. She was only about ten at the time so didn't have much experience driving horses without help! The mule would kick at Old Bob if she came close to him. Finally, the two trotted up to a small house where there was a barrel of water. Old Beauty got her head into the barrel and was drinking but Edna couldn't make her get it out. A young couple lived there. The man got a rope and put it on Beauty and made her go with Edna and started the mule following after them.

It was really dark by then. When Edna got back to the road and started toward camp, she kept wishing she could be back at camp—not really frightened but pretty much on the alert. Then she heard a horse coming down the road. It knickered and she thought, "That sounds like Old Lil's knicker." But it was so dark, she could not actually see it at all. She sensed a horse nearby, turning around toward her. A man reached out and took hold of her arm. It was Grandad! Edna almost cried with relief! He told her then that some men who had been burning a fire guard close by the camp had told him a little girl had been kidnapped the week before and they still had not found the man but did find the little girl where he left her. When they got back to camp, Grandma was crying hysterically and was so relieved to see them!

33

After that, one child was never sent alone on any errand that would take him out of sight of the camp. They decided there was safety in numbers and if two couldn't go together, neither would go. So another lesson was learned on the trail.

11- GOING BACK TO KANSAS!

Going back to the west, the families stopped in some of the same places they had camped while going east. This provoked a lot of questions at the livery stables on why the group turned around.

There had been a big blizzard farther west. They came upon cattle that had died in the storm and fence corners were still piled high with snow where there was anything for the snow to drift against. They were thankful they had not been in that part when the blizzard was in progress. It had been very bad. At a ranch where they camped for the night, Grandad watered the horses and the man wouldn't take any money for the fodder their horses ate—only for the grain. Next morning when they were ready to leave, the boy who lived there asked his dad to ask Grandad how much would he sell our dog, Old Black, for. Since they had been so nice to us, Grandad said he would give them Old Black. Uncle Wiley was only about nine and he considered Old Black his dog! He was heartsick at leaving him behind but could say nothing. Grandad said that without the hound that had been stolen, Black wasn't much good alone because it took both of them to make a hunting team. So they left without Black and Wiley was sad. About three in the afternoon, Wiley looked out of the wagon and could see a black speck down the road behind them. It seemed to be moving and Wiley said he hoped it was Old Black. Sure enough, it was! He was dragging a short rope, chewed off at the end! He had found his family and was really joyful! Grandad said it was hard to know which was happier, the boy or the dog! One night when camped out in one of the towns they had stayed in while coming east, Grandad was standing outside the wagon looking around when a dog ran up to him and jumped up on him, wiggling and licking and acting so glad. Yes, it was Old Blue! The boy that had stolen her didn't know Grandad was the owner. The boy approached her, calling her "Queen." Grandad asked "What do you think you're doing?" He faced the boy and told him who he was—the owner! The boy lost no time in disappearing! The two greyhounds were overjoyed at seeing each other again. They caught many a jackrabbit and quite a few coyotes after that!

Traveling along the main road one Sunday morning, the family encountered wind blowing so hard they had to stop, for fear the top-heavy wagons would blow over. They put guy ropes on the wagons to tie them to the ground and put the three youngest children on quilts on the ground with another quilt tied over them, afraid to use the wagon for shelter in the fear it would topple and roll. Grandad saw a farm house about a mile or so on lower ground to the south so told Grandma he was going to see if they could stay by that barn until the wind went down.

He rode down there and found the man to be Lemon Sutton, whose wife and children were in Dodge City visiting her father. He said, sure, the family was welcome to come down and stay right in the house. So he came back with Grandad to the camp and helped him bring the wagons and the family to his place. They put the wagons in safe shelter and stabled the horses. He insisted that everyone come right into the house, cook on his stove and sleep in the house. He was wonderful to everyone!

12- WELCOME TO THE OASIS

When Grandad told him they were headed back to Hamilton County to buy another place, Mr. Sutton told him about a school section of land that one could have a quarter-section free just by settling on it and improving it! It was just five miles from his place, to the south. The very next morning, Lemon Sutton took Grandad and Grandma to see the ground. Both liked it so well, they decided on the spot to move the wagons down there.

Grandma said it looked better than Hamilton County to her! There was an empty house just across the road from the "school quarter" and a big red barn. Lemon, as he insisted they call him, said it would be all right to live in the house, so they moved their things into it! Grandad had to put a few glass panes in some of the broken windows but after that is was quite nice. A family named Brown had lived there but had gone back to another, greener place they had liked better. The creek was only a mile south of the house and the horses could drink there. There was a bigger, two-story house down near the creek that was also empty. It had a big cellar and a well drilled in the cellar, with a pump on it. The family could pump water there and haul it to their new home until Grandad could get a well put in.

Lemon Sutton was always willing to help Grandad in any way he could and the two remained friends for life! Although the Tullis farm finally went to heirs by another name after the sons, Wiley and Walter, passed on, some Sutton land is still held by Sutton descendents. The town of Ensign, southwest of Dodge City, bore the Sutton name on many of its businesses up through the 1930's. As well as being a farmer, Lemon was an astute businessman and opened a lively trade territory that flourished until the depression of the 1930's.

After settling into a new home in Gray County, the Tullis family still had to get back to Hamilton County to reclaim their livestock. That required taking a wagon and the older children to help bring the cattle to Gray County. Hubbard's were greatly surprised to see their friends and to know they had settled no farther away than Gray County, less than a hundred miles, where heavy rich soil almost begged to be plowed! The Tullises had found their oasis!

Grandad looked at the stock and saw he would have to build a wagon to carry the little calves because baby calves couldn't travel that far on foot. He loaded the things they had left at Len's and said he would have to bring the two older children back again to get the cattle. There was just too much to handle in one trip. By the time they got back, there were five baby calves and two colts to bring plus all the cattle to be driven. They even brought Edna along to help as much as she could. Grandma and Grace and Walter were very glad to see them when they finally got back. The abundance of grass and water at the creek was a real blessing. Grandma and Grandad commenced plowing and planting almost at once and, as soon as the crops were planted, Grandad got someone to drill a well on the school quarter and put a windmill up. As soon as he had a place built to live in, they moved onto the school quarter because the contract stated that the homesteader must "Improve the property!" Improving meant building; that is how the term "proving up a claim" came to be.

13- MIXED-UP CATTLE

Western cowboys would drive a big herd through the countryside and some of the weaker cows would fall behind because they couldn't travel any farther. They would be left to regain their strength or to die, whichever happened, and if they survived, they would be picked up on the next trip through. Those cows were wild and not used to being handled by people on foot. They would fight at the slightest provocation and would sometimes get in with the herd of milk cows. Whoever went after the cows at milking time had to chase away the wild cows. That was often very hard to do.

One night when Grandad's milk cows were shut up in the corral, about midnight he heard bawling of cattle and knew there was something bothering his cows. He thought it could be neighbor Sam Batemans'cattle. Bateman had eight or ten cows.

Grandad and Grandma went toward the barn where they saw a spotted cow, which they thought was Bateman's. It was not. It was a wild cow that decided to send them flying. She put her head down and started for them. Grandad yelled at Grandma to run; but he said later, that she flew instead. He managed to get the cow after him, rather than after Grandma, and when she came too close, he had to take refuge in an old wagon with a broken wheel.. The cow kept him pinned in the wagon for an hour before she went back to the barn. He finally managed to get back to the house. Next morning, on horseback and with pitchfork in hand, he chased the old cow a mile away. She got into the neighbor's herd and he also got tired of having to chase her away before he could go near his cattle. She got nice and fat during several months so he finally shot her and butchered her for beef. Some of the other farmers did the same thing with wild cows that hung around their herds. It seemed the right thing to do since no one had any control over the wild cows and they were a danger to anyone on foot…

Grandad was careful to teach both his wife and his children about the habits of animals. One such pearl of wisdom was that "a bull closes his eyes when charging but a cow keeps her eyes open." The message to be learned was that you could sidestep the charge of a bull if you kept your wits about you and remain perfectly safe because he would go right on by you. Not so with a cow. Cows aimed and charged with both eyes open! To protect yourself, get behind something she couldn't break!

14-LESSONS LEARNED ON THE PRAIRIE

I should point out that the self-reliance of the Tullis children didn't just "happen." Their parents relied on them to do every assigned job and to do it well. Jessie was nine years old when Aunt Grace was born in Hamilton County, 1888. Since the mid-wife assisted only with the delivery and left early the next morning, it was up to nine-year-old Jessie, the oldest child, to prepare the meals—no small task, and to help Grandad with the washing! He heated the water and poured it from boiler to tub while she did the actual scrubbing on the board. They put everything through one rinse and then hung the clothes outside on wire fences to dry. The whole process was repeated two years later when Uncle Walter was born. Edna and Wiley were a little older and had learned to help with many chores by that time.

One incident that was absolutely chilling happened to Grandma when baby Grace was just six months old. Grandma had put her outside the door on a quilt to get some sunshine. The older children had all gone with Grandad to help him with the work for that day. Everyone always had a job to do! Grandma would check on Grace from time to time, to be sure she didn't get off the quilt. That was the biggest danger, she thought. Alas, it wasn't! Looking out the door, Grandma saw a cougar, lying nearby, twitching its tail, getting ready to spring on the baby! With tea towel in hand—because that was all she had for self-defense, Grandma ran out the door waving the towel and screaming at the cougar. It retreated and slunk away toward the river. Grandma grabbed Grace and got back inside the house before breaking down into sobs, almost hysterical. Grandad and the older kids had heard a faint scream carried on the wind and thought something must be terribly wrong. They returned to the house to find Grandma still crying and thanking the Lord for giving her the reminder to look out the door! Grace was unaware of the cougar, naturally, but loved to hear "the cougar story" when she got a little older. My mother repeated it to me as well.

15- GROWING NEIGHBORHOOD RELATIONS

It was 1894 when the Tullis family settled in Gray County. Jessie was a teen-ager and had begun to attract beaus. Two young fellows about her age, were vying to take her to a neighborhood party where there would be dancing, food and much socializing. However, she got a chance to go to Syracuse to visit her former teacher, a woman she absolutely adored, so the two young men were greatly disappointed. It was shortly after that when she met a young Irishman named McCauley who came up from the Cimarron River ranch of his stepfather and mother, where he was known for his skills at breaking and training horses.

His grandparents and uncles lived in the neighborhood along the banks of Crooked Creek, only a few miles east of the Tullis family. He sometimes stayed on a weekend and played for any dances that might be going on. An accomplished "fiddler," he had taught himself to play the violin at an early age. He also played the pump organ, self-taught, and could play any tune if someone would hum it for him. You could say that he had "an ear for music." He had red, curly hair and green eyes and was known to be an excellent dancer when he got a chance to put the violin aside for a few moments. After Jessie had danced with "Kid" McCauley two or three times, she decided that he was the one she would most like to have come courting her! They became a "pair" and in February,1898, they were married at the Tullis home in Gray County. He had apparently got the nickname, "Kid" down on the Cimarron, where, at age sixteen, he had become "the" horse breaker and trainer of good reputation. But Jessie always called him Will.

They found a quarter of land near her parents that could be owned just for "proving-up" and began building a soddy. That was another name for the sod house. It had a board roof, with tarpaper laid carefully over the boards before being covered with sod. There was also a big south window to let in sunshine in the winter! The walls were plastered inside with white plaster. Outside, as close to the house as possible was a windmill and tank. They had learned from Grandad that it was more important to have your water supply close to those who would use it. You could always pipe it downhill to the cattle because cattle didn't care whether their water was cold or not as long as the supply was plentiful! Building a soddy is a lot of work, especially if you are working a full day to herd your cattle, plant your fields, gather your harvest. Going from cowboys to full-time farmers to house builders is not easy. Life was still primitive and still hard. So Will and Jessie moved into the old Way Station near Crooked Creek where an old rock crossing marked the Jones & Plummer trail; the wagon-wheel ruts are still visible but overgrown with grass.

Somehow it didn't bother the young couple that the last stationmaster had been fatally stabbed by an assailant in the night and hung up on a hook inside the door of the dugout! The man's murderer was never found and the owners of the freight line abandoned the premises soon afterward. So Will and Jessie lived in the old way-station dugout during their first year of marriage while they worked on their sod mansion! It proved to be a good plan; for the snow was very deep that winter and their cattle had the benefit of the trees along Crooked Creek for shelter! They had all the firewood nearby that anyone could want—just for the cutting, so there was no need to gather cow chips, a job they both knew well from years of prairie life.

My dad, Will McCauley, was a member of the McCauley clan that migrated by covered wagon train and by railroad from Illinois to Kansas early in 1879. Andrew J. McCauley and wife, Mary Brown, had four grown sons, J.C. Fremont, Charley, Forrest and Andrew Junior, along with two daughters, Helen and Belle---who was really Arinda Arabela, but everyone knew her as "Belle." Belle had a husband, Howard Gilchrist, an ordained preacher; Helen had an out-of-wedlock son, Willie, four years old, named for his father, Wilbur Evans, an Irish Catholic whom the family absolutely disdained. In fact, they had moved from Ohio to Illinois five years earlier to get their daughter away from the man because she was determined to marry him, in spite of his "undesirable" religion! McCauley's were strict Congregationalists.

16-THE OHIO COLONY

The Ohio Colony had originated in Zanesville, Ohio, near where the grandfather, Patrick McCauley, had lived since 1863. Before that date, he had dwelt in Bucks County, Pennsylvania, where six of the twelve children had been born.

The great-grandfather, Phillip McCauley, had been "driven from Ireland" in the *Irish Rebellion of 1798* and had fought in the War of 1812. He had married Mary Brown, a Pennsylvania native of German origin, who lived to be 101 years of age. They had produced three children, of whom Patrick was second. He lived from 1802 to 1871.

Patrick's seventh child, Andrew Jackson McCauley, was born in 1833 and grew up in the wilderness of Tiffin Township, Ohio, on Section 21. It was in Tiffin Township that Andrew Jackson McCauley met and married another Mary Brown, this one of English origin, in March, 1854.

Andrew J. and Mary Brown produced a daughter, Helen, my grandma, in 1855. John Charles Fremont in 1857, Arinda Arabella in 1859, Wesley B, in 1861, Andrew, Junior, in 1863, Charles Dwinn in 1865, Forrest Henry in 1867 and Nellie Grace in 1870. The last baby lived to be only a year old and the middle son, Andrew, Jr., died of typhoid at age 22 in Kansas. Wesley chose Florida and never set foot in Kansas, as far as anyone could tell.

Andrew J. and his wife, Mary, with six of their adult children, a son-in-law and four-year-old grandson, Willie, joined the Colony as it came along the Ohio river through southern Illinois in 1879—in

February, but the exact date is unknown or was never told to me. They brought wagons, numerous horses, feed, seed, furniture and enough utensils to "get by" in their new home on the Kansas prairie—a distance of some 1300 miles. They had never tasted the fresh air of Kansas nor felt its biting winter gales; they came on faith and the word of two, young, single men who had come the year before as scouts for the organizer, a man named John Jobling, a native of England.

The pair, Ben Haywood , a native of Maine, and Elijah Hutchinson, a transplanted Kentuckian, had been all the way west to Kansas and south to Abilene, Texas, on their previous excursion westward. Those two adventurers advised Jobling and his promoter—a man named Jed Copeland—that Kansas was the place to go. There was land to be homesteaded just for staking a claim and grassland in abundance for those who wanted to raise cattle! They had seen Kansas in a wet year so did not realize how scant the rain could become in a dry year. In those days, land companies actually promoted settling of the west and made their money by organizing wagon trains and railroad trips to take people to the new lands of promise.

Sometimes the promise was greater than the fulfillment if the promoter happened to have "a way with words." Jobling, Haywood and Hutchinson all were men of their word and came the 1,300 miles with the group. They all lived in the vicinity of Crooked Creek, 25 miles southwest of the present Dodge City, until the end of their lives. They were men of good reputation and character and had the respect of their peers in the area.

Settling of such a Colony wasn't an easy thing! Most of the members were not farmers, but tradesmen with a skill. They didn't know anything about planting and harvesting, or literally wresting a living from the soil. Most had only worked at menial jobs during their young lives and had no "savings" to fall back on if things went sour. They had heard the organizers' term "free land, just for living on it and proving up a claim," and it didn't occur to them how hard that would be for a five-year period!

The U.S. government didn't make any special stipulations for homesteaders other than that they had to build on a claim and live there for five consecutive years. Nothing was mentioned about having a cash reserve for "hard times," or having farming skills to be able to plant and reap some kind of food for themselves and their animals! So a great many of the young couples who came simply ran out of money during the first year of what proved to be a terrible drought. No rains fell. No grass grew. Everything stayed brown all summer long. Many seeds they had so hopefully put into the ground simply didn't sprout. Those that sprouted died soon after. The summer of 1879 turned dismally sour when the Ohioans, used to plentiful rain, realized that Kansas was a far cry from what they had believed it to be.

While some families had settled on the banks of Crooked Creek, others had gone four or five miles farther into a natural basin that came to be known as the Artesian Valley. They laid out a town of several square blocks and even established a post office. One of the founders, Cyrus Atkinson, had a baby daughter, Pearl, who had been sick on the Colony's arrival in Dodge City. The baby and mother had stayed in Dodge while the father had gone on out to the valley to build on his claim. For awhile, the baby seemed to improve but that didn't last. She died at age sixteen months, the first victim of the difficult journey to the new land!

The community grieved with the Atkinson's over their loss and decided to honor baby Pearl by naming the new town after her. While still back in Ohio, the settlers had planned to name their first town "Sunshine." With Pearl's death, they decided to name it "Pearlette." Sadly, baby Pearl's demise was the first of many baby deaths that first year. Almost nothing was known about sanitation, boiling the drinking water, or preventing flies from settling on food. So it happened that babies got dysentery and died of dehydration very rapidly. This made the establishment of a cemetery an urgent matter, even before the building of a church.

By the following summer, four-year-old Willie, who was to be my dad, was the youngest child left standing in the Colony. The town of Pearlette had really tough times from the start. A man named Addison Bennett and his partner, Howard Lowery, had actually brought a printing press to Kansas on their migration! They built a sod house at the Pearlette townsite. The six Atkinson's shared the house and used it to publish the first newspaper on April 15, 1879, calling it the Call. In its lead editorial, the editor stated that Kansas had presented many more obstacles than any Ohioan had been able to foresee.

Bennett was appointed postmaster of an official U.S. Post Office and the mail was delivered by stagecoach once weekly. In May, Bennett was able to report that about twenty new families had located in the vicinity during the month! The little cluster of soddies that marked Pearlette hardly distinguished the landscape and it was easy to miss the town entirely during the night! That fact led to much confusion when a birth occurred and the guide for the midwife became as lost as if he were a tourist!

The first child born in the Ohio Colony belonged to Mrs.Dunk Arter. She was in serious labor about 1 a.m. Dunk sent his neighbor, Billy Burnshoe, to get Mrs. Lawson, the midwife. Alas, the two got lost and finally came to the <u>Call</u> office, two miles south of the Arter soddie! Dunk went looking for another neighbor, leaving his wife alone. By the time all the lost parties got their bearings and determined where the Arter house was, Mrs. Arter had delivered her own son and was holding him in her arms, three hours old! Fortunately, most of the folks involved had a sense of humor and could see the funny side of getting lost in their own neighborhood.

Although the Arter baby was called the first child of the Ohio Colony, he was not the first Anglo baby to be born in what is now Meade County. That honor went to John Eliason, son of Andor and Helena Eliason, a Norwegian couple who had come down from Minnesota. Andor had come alone, leaving his wife and three daughters in more civilized surroundings until he could establish his farm. He was already settled when the Ohio Colony got to the area and had previously had some encounters with a few Indians before he got well settled. One such encounter left Andor without any feed for his livestock. He had hidden his brand new wood-burning cookstove beneath a quickly fashioned stack of hay when another settler had warned him that Indians were coming that way. That settler urged him not to stay there alone but to take refuge up on Crooked Creek with some of the Ohio Colony. He followed the advice. When he returned to his claim, he found the haystacks all burned and his supplies scattered. The cookstove had withstood the heat of the burning hay and, after a "polishing" with stove black, worked as well as ever.

The town of Pearlette began to feel the hard times almost from the beginning! Crooked Creek went dry from its head up in Gray County down to where it connected with Spring Creek south of the present-day Meade. The wind seemed to blow constantly and so hard that it could make anyone miserable. Over that entire span of valley, almost no hay was cut that summer. It was estimated to be less than 50 tons. Such was the initiation of the Ohio Colony to life in Kansas!

By July, 1879, many of the young couples with children had run out of money. Some had written relatives in Ohio, asking for assistance. The men began to look for day labor any place they could find. Two went to Dodge City to work in a brickyard; another became a baker in Dodge. Dunk Arter hired out as a sheep shearer at a ranch down on the Cimarron River; Jed Copeland, one of the organizers, became a brakeman on the Santa Fe. Sickness and injury took a toll. As early as June, some packages from Ohio had already arrived in Pearlette. By July, the Lowery family moved back to Kansas City where employment was more probable. The Thompson's decided to return to Ohio in August. So, the ranks were broken and the troops began a retreat. Little Pearlette was finally abandoned. By October, 1880, most of the Pearlette dwellers had gone elsewhere and the only buildings occupied were one store and two homes. When Bennett moved on to publish another paper in another location, John Jobling took over the post-office and managed to keep it alive until February,1887. People in Fowler had complained about poor postal service at Pearlette! Fowler City had just been designated as a division town on the Rock Island Railroad. That did it! Mail service to Pearlette was discontinued and Fowler became the address of choice. Jobling was quick to see the signs of the times and moved both his store and house to Fowler, a distance of six miles.

Other towns had sprung up during the early 1880's. Beside Fowler and Wilburn, there were Spring Lake and Meade Center. They became the trading centers and thrived for awhile. It was really the location of the Rock Island Railroad that determined which three towns would survive and which would fail. Likewise, the farmers who actually had farmed before coming to Kansas, found it possible to hang on to their claims and grub a living from the soil. However, many of them had to find work off the farm during the leanest years—the McCauley's being among those! They got work on the railroad as well as on the "76 Ranch," owned by John Conrad, a prosperous operator.

At age eleven, my dad went to live on the Cimarron River ranch of his stepfather, Hervy Forbes. The Rock Island was crossing Seward County. Dad drove spikes with a sledge-hammer that summer, keeping those calluses on his palms for many years! He could have worked full time but, by age sixteen, he'd had enough railroad experience and turned to breaking horses for a living—more exciting! No two days and no two horses were ever the same!

17- THE BLIZZARD OF 1886

Many tales have been told about the blizzard of '86. Probably some are true and others not. It was terrible for those who lived to tell of it! It began on January first and lasted through the fifth, sifting every nook and cranny full of fine, white powder in a temperature 20 degrees below zero. As if that weren't enough, a second storm hit on the thirteenth and lasted over 24 hours. People took refuge wherever they happened to be at the time.

The poor cattle were not so lucky. At twenty below zero, a cutting snowstorm and a driving wind can kill animals by freezing or by suffocating them. The powdery snow, inhaled, brought on rapid death. Many of them froze to death. The twenty percent of range cattle that found shelter—a ditch, a bluff, or a few trees, managed to survive. Seventy-five to eighty percent just drifted with the winds until they stumbled and fell. Other cattle piled up over them. That was how they were found when the air finally cleared—all piled up, some still standing, frozen in place. Dad said it really was true that you could walk across the Cimarron River on the level, just walking on the carcasses of the dead livestock.

Clarence and Carl Haywood's mother, Mattie, had a tale to tell about the storm. She could laugh about it years later but said it was no laughing matter at the time. She was trying to prove up her own claim when she came up from Kentucky while yet single. Then she married Charley, a brother to Ben, and still tried to keep her claim going. As luck would have it, she and a girlfriend had gone down to her claim north of Fowler on that fateful day. Seeing they were trapped for the duration of the storm, Mattie said her first thought was to try to save the milk cow that was out in a makeshift shed. Seeing no way to give her protection, the two women simply brought the cow into the dugout to endure the storm. It was a slightly smelly operation but both they and the cow survived!

Mattie was full of stories about her life after coming to Kansas as a young woman. She had grown up in a red brick mansion, complete with servants and much finery in the rolling Kentucky hills. Then a twist of fate brought her west to Kansas to assist her dad, Elijah, in running his road ranch. Later she fell for Charley Haywood and married him. I knew her from my earliest childhood memories up until the day she died. Her only daughter, Nettie, was one of my dearest friends. Nettie married Paul Younger, a Quaker preacher, who was called to California in the early thirties. We kept in touch all our lives, mostly by letters, after she moved to the West Coast. Nettie and I, as girls, loved to get her mother to telling stories about her first years in Kansas. She was an enthralling storyteller!

One of her "best" and funniest stories was about how she learned to toss cow chips into the range while cooking. In Kentucky they had burned wood and the servants stoked the fire. In Kansas, you either learned to toss cow chips or you didn't cook. She said at first she put on gloves for the job; that soon proved to be too much trouble. She learned of necessity to use two fingers to pick up the chip and flip it into the fire! Before long, she could wipe her fingers on her apron and go on handling the food she was cooking. After all, cooking would kill any impurities. Then, she added with a twinkle in her eye, "I found out spices were good to cover up any strange odor the chips might impart!" The shortcut in handling the cow chips probably was practiced in most of those pioneer kitchens. After all, there were only so many hours of day!

If the blizzard of '86 was tough for the cattlemen—and it was, the other terrible hazard to add to the list that included drought and blizzard was the always-present risk of *prairie fire.* That struck fear in the hearts of both cattleman and farmer!

Mattie Haywood's brother, Willie Hutchinson, had come up from Kentucky to help their dad run his Road Ranche. George Fowler founded his town just four miles from that road ranch and the town succeeded in getting the Rock Island Railway to come its way, forever ruining the dreams of all "freighters" including Hutchinson. Willie had thought a few months before that the railroad was coming to Wilburn, southwest of Dodge City and had bought property there. He had just built an expensive set of buildings—a barn, granary, hay storage, plus much fencing. Alas, a prairie fire started somewhere near Dodge City and roared across country almost thirty miles to the Wilburn area. It jumped creeks and ran around the occasional plowed field in its path. A strong wind whipped up burning cow chips and rolled them along the leading edge of the blaze up to ¼ mile of the main blaze. It was described in the April14,1887, issue of the Fowler Graphic as a "scene of grandeur and magificence when darkness fell." For Hutchinson and others who lost their grass, cattle, horses and many buildings, it was a scene of financial ruin. Some of them never recovered their losses. It was a story often repeated on the dry prairie.

18- UNCLE BEN

I remember Uncle Ben Haywood in particular because, being a bachelor, he used to come to our house for Sunday dinner on invitation. I loved to hear him say words like "butter" because he always dropped the "r" and it came out "buttah." One of my great entertainments was to sit and listen to him tell yarns about his early days in Maine. I soon figured out that probably everyone in Maine said "buttah" for butter. The word, door, was always "doh-ah" and floor was always "floh-ah"—for Uncle Ben never lost his New England accent! Uncle Ben was a source of great delight to me and I to him, apparently, for he liked to spoil little girls by bringing them candy when he came to dinner. He wasn't really my uncle but everyone called him "Uncle Ben" so I did, too. He was a man of impeccable honesty and was quite well read for his day. My mother said that many of the ladies of the community considered him to be the most eligible bachelor and he stayed that way—a bachelor. Someone told a tale in his brother's family that Ben had had a true love in Maine but had stayed away too long. Finally when he got back there, he had found her to be married to someone else. We never found out the truth for Uncle Ben never discussed it. He was a fine example of the Puritan Ethic!

Back to the Colony, the settlers particularly liked the banks of Crooked Creek southwest of Dodge City. They hit the ground with enthusiasm and soon had their dugouts built on the quarters of land they had selected for homesteading. Everyone over 21 was allowed to claim land if he would erect some kind of dwelling and live in it five years. The community took form fairly rapidly and, before long, was known through the area as "The Ohio Colony." They built a school on one quarter-section which could double as a church called the First Congregational Church of Crooked Creek, the first church in the present Meade County. It was called Ford County at the time—Meade County's survey was not complete until 1885.

Unfortunately, typhoid fever and dysentery ran through the group. By the end of the first year, the infants had all died. The youngest child left was Willie, the four-year-old grandson whom I would later call "Dad." Those early deaths required that a cemetery be built. One corner of a McCauley quarter was used for that purpose and one-third of that plot soon held many little wooden and iron crosses. The first two years were hard years and sad ones, especially for the women. In some cases, their loss was their first-born child. More than thirty infants were buried that first year!

Aunt Belle's husband, Howard, soon had Sunday services organized. In the summer months he held tent services in the Emerson grove—a big grove of trees that had been planted by a cattleman named Emerson who had moved on to Clark County where the rock outcroppings were more to his liking as a natural shelter for herds of cattle. People from the Artesian Valley, about four miles south, came up to the meetings. They would bring food, cook out and spend the night, breaking camp at daylight the next day to head for home. Sunday tent services were a big event.

One little boy from the valley, named George Foster, loved to come up to the tent meetings. He and my dad, Will, would play non-stop every waking moment because neither of them got to see other children at home. Typhoid and dysentery had taken all the babies, so George and Will were the lone warriors of their generation. It's not too surprising that they remained life-long friends and were always joyful to see each other at any community function where they happened to meet. They both lived into their eighties and were uncommonly healthy. A Foster daughter—I'm not sure which, married Captain French, another settler in the valley who carried his Civil War designation of Captain as long as he lived. They moved to Oklahoma territory, settling about where the present day Woodward is located. Some of their descendents remain there.

"Cap" French was a colorful figure. My mother told me many tales of adventure that involved "Cap" French's going out to rescue some pitiful settler or traveler in distress. He seldom carried a water jug but always carried a flask of "something stronger." His reasoning was that, if the going got really rough, he would need a lot more than water to get him through. He was known as a crack marksman and hunter and he had an uncanny sense of direction without benefit of compasses or maps. You could say he was almost a legendary character, I suppose.

Helen McCauley, my grandmother, married Hervy Forbes, one of the Ohio colony that went on to settle a ranch in Seward County on the Cimarron River, where the town of Arkalon sprang up. My dad was only nineteen when his mother died. It must have hurt him terribly that her obituary contained no mention of him as a son. Out-of-wedlock children were often unmentioned because of the stigma of their birth, sadly. My dad never seemed to be bitter about his treatment. He loved his two siblings, Maude and Walter Forbes. Maude married and left while still in her teens but Uncle Walter lived in Liberal till the day he died. He and my dad would visit periodically through the years and would enjoy recounting their youth along the Cimarron River. They had much "high adventure" according to their tales! My only regret is that I didn't write down a lot of what they told of their doings. It would have made a good book. They had a talent for inventive mischief!

J.C.F. McCauley, or Uncle Fremont as I knew him, was a dour man, very inventive and very materialistic. He built a machine shop and made the tools he needed in order to get ahead. He bought what was apparently the first steam engine thresher in the county and soon had farmers lining up to get on his list of threshing clients. He employed his brothers and close neighbors and worked terribly long hours. His belief was that daylight was wasted if you didn't use it for working! He married Mary Bateman, daughter of an Ohio family. Since they produced no children, they adopted her nephews and a niece, Jim, Joe and Cora Schmid. They were such bad parents that Cora ran away at the first opportunity and Jim and Joe were not far behind her. Jim was the only one who came back to see Fremont in his old age. He was a tall, dark, good-looking man with a keen sense of humor. Jim was not eligible for the draft of World War II because of his asthma. He rented farmland in Gove County, and prospered but never married. We were best friends till his death in the early 1970's.

Fremont disinherited his own brother, Forrest, who lived on some of his land, leaving the place instead to a traveling preacher by the name of Bridgewater who had held revivals in the area. Needless to say, Mr. Bridgewater never returned to hold more meetings after the "windfall" of ten quarters of rich farmland. My mother said that the McCauley's deserved to be disinherited because they didn't stand up to Fremont and Mary to defend those three adopted kids who were so abused. No mention of the three children was made in Fremont's will—a document which had been re-written just weeks before his death—supposedly with the aid of the preacher! Bridgewater took a "loan" on the bequeathed land and never repaid it. A big beneficiary was a lawyer in Dodge City who made the loan at a fraction of the land's value! Fremont's brother, Uncle Forrest, and his son, Andrew, were the losers in the will! They were living on Andrew J. McCauley, Sr.'s farm with the prior understanding that it was to go to Forrest at his eldest brother's death. Fremont was in his eighties and not mentally capable of re-writing his will. I saw him on a fairly regular basis and thought how fast he was failing. I had no idea that the preacher was scheming to get him to change his will...Forrest and Andrew were suddenly without a home and had to vacate the premises within a very short time. The family pulled up stakes and moved to Oklahoma where the living in 1939 was just as bleak as it was in Kansas. Andrew and his wife, Edna, whom I dearly loved, had six children. A seventh was born in Oklahoma in 1939. Edna had a sister in Oklahoma and she had been born and reared there. Fortunately for them, they moved on to California where they were fully employed in the wartime economy of the 1940's. They lived at Vallejo for many years. Most of Andrew's children still live in that area. Their names were Jeanne, Edward, Robert, Nathan, Mary, Martha and Ruth. All were blond, blue-eyed and well-behaved, pretty children—very bright, and all reared in the Christian faith.

Aunt Belle and Uncle Howard had three children, Nellie, Harold and Mary. Nellie's son, Ralph Gaston, died young as did her sister. Her husband, Alec Gaston, had deserted Nellie and their little Ralph didn't thrive. He died, bedfast, at age sixteen. No one knew the exact cause of his ailment. After losing Ralph, Nellie married Will Ellson, a man who worked for Uncle Charlie. Will was a kind, generous, Christian man entirely devoted to Nellie. The loss of her son and her sister, Mary, seemed to cause her a great deal of depression. She was a temperamental lady, given to sudden anger. I never really understood her volatile ways.

Harold married Eunice, the daughter of a Christian minister from Michigan, named John Henry Klopfenstein. Eunice was a dear and we kept in touch as long as she lived. Most of the Gilchrist children and their descendents still live in the Oregon and Washington vicinity. They were named Carole, Duane, Don, and Naomi and were very handsome children. Carole's twin,Corlyn, was stillborn and was buried at the Concord Church Cemetery about 12 miles southwest of Dodge City. Eunice had another baby girl, Corliss, when they lived in Liberal. She was blue and never lived to breathe. Her burial was at Liberal Cemetery.

Howard Gilchrist preached all his life until he died. He found that the Methodists needed circuit riders and became a Methodist preacher. He was a pretty good preacher and Aunt Belle was certainly a good disciple. She would preach about salvation to anyone who would listen to her. I can remember her standing at a window in their house and remarking that "The Lord may come this very night." She died in 1936 and was buried near her husband in the McCauley Cemetery north of Fowler.

Wesley B. McCauley married a woman named Laura Spangler and moved to Florida. As far as I know, he never set foot on Kansas soil.

Andrew, Jr., died unmarried at age 22, of typhoid.

The youngest child, Nellie Grace, lived only one year, dying in 1871 in Ohio.

Uncle Charley never married but established a comfortable home after he graduated from Kansas State College. He was a leader in the community and very well respected by everyone who knew him. He had been a board member of almost every public establishment in Fowler and people sought his opinion on many things. He died at age sixty-eight on his farm north of Fowler, Kansas; having multiple strokes and spending his last three years in a wheelchair. I was always in awe of him. He was very wise.

Uncle Forrest married Flora Davis in Topeka, Kansas, in 1892. Part of his adult life was spent employed by the Santa Fe in Topeka. Later he moved to Colfax, Iowa, working as a bookkeeper in a general store. In 1898, he moved back to the farm when his father's health began to wane. Uncle Forrest and Aunt Flo, whom I loved dearly, had four children who lived to grow up, Andrew, Stella, Albert and Mildred. I felt a deep affection for my cousins and maintained lifelong contact with them. Edna and I kept in touch till the end of her life.

19- HAPPY CHILDHOOD IN A CLOSE-KNIT COMMUNITY

Since my grandparents on the McCauley side were not living, Dad's mother having died before he married, it was pretty natural that I would develop my first close relationships with my mother's sisters, Aunt Edna and Aunt Grace. Grace was only ten years older than I and she spoiled me terribly. She would swoop me up into the saddle with her and we would take off at a full gallop for whatever task was at hand. I loved Aunt Grace to the point of adoration. There was only one time that I did not. That was the night that her son, Loyde, was born!

I was twelve years old—how well I remember! My dad had taken me to the doctor at Fowler to have my tonsils removed. We came home that eight miles in a horse-drawn buggy and I was miserable. My throat was screaming at me for attention. I wanted a drink but knew it would hurt so badly that I couldn't swallow anything. I wanted, most of all, my mother! If I could just live to get home, I thought, my mother would make it "all better." She always did. We finally got home; dad carried me into the house and to my bed. My mother was bustling about her darling and I felt better already, just knowing she was there. We hadn't been home more than an hour when here came Uncle Paskel, Aunt Grace's husband. He was frantic. Would Jessie please go to be with Grace, quick! She was in labor. He was on his way to Meade—18 miles, by horse, to summon the doctor! Of course my mother would go. She was the leading "mid-wife" of the community and seldom missed a birth. Grace was her baby sister! She handed me off like a "hot potato" –or so I felt, and grabbed her already-packed bag, dashed to the barn

66

and mounted her horse –and away she went. Her parting words were, "Dad will look after you, honey."

Poor Dad tried his best to comfort me and actually sat up with me all night. But I was a bit spoiled, being an only child, and I felt terribly abused by a horrible little baby who would be so impudent as to choose that night to be born. I resolved to hate that baby at first sight. I was going to resent him forever. Dad and I got through the night. It probably was not easy for him but he didn't complain. He was an adoring, doting father who was going to be both mother and father or whatever the situation demanded.

Next morning he fixed me some very thin, cornmeal mush, with sugar and milk and he had me completely happy by the time my mother came home, tired to the bone, announcing that the baby was a boy and they were going to call him Loyde. I resolved I would never like Loyde and could hardly wait to meet him to tell him so. However, I soon found Loyde to be a very interesting, alert little character who smiled, gooed and cooed and was generally agreeable. By the time he was a year old, he fascinated me and he became my favorite "toy," much more fun than any old doll. The tonsillectomy and pain were history. Loyde turned out to be my favorite cousin—I had several favorites—and we had a real bond.

My mother often went to a neighbor's at the time of a birthing. All the ladies of the community seemed to have great faith in her to deliver them. My dad said it was because she always cleaned the whole place and fixed everything up for the coming week before she returned home! She would scrub, clean, do the washing and the baking or whatever she could to lighten the load for the new mother.

One family in particular had a baby almost every year. Dad said you could tell it was spring because they would come for his wife to clean their place and deliver the new one! He thought maybe they planned it that way! She even took their mattresses outside and wiped them with kerosene to kill the bedbugs! No doubt they did appreciate the fact that she was a very industrious housekeeper as well as a good cook and midwife. But she always scolded Dad for his remarks, "Oh, Will, don't be so foolish! Nobody would plan a baby just for that!" He said he wasn't so sure. I always listened intently to their discussion of neighbors!

Glossary of terms, Chapters 18-19

Puritan Ethic- *a doctrine taught in New England by the first Colonists, affirming that, if a man feared God, worked hard, was moderate in all things and didn't spend the principal, he would overcome the hazards of a perverse growing season, beget children and die in old age surrounded by those same Christian offspring, a full granary and the certain knowledge of eternal salvation. It was a Code of Conduct that prevailed in much of the settlement of the West—Kansas in particular, as it had in the northeastern colonies.*

Kansas State College of Agriculture and Applied Science- *a tax supported institution that later became Kansas State University.*

Irish Rebellion of 1798- *Uprising of Irish peasant farmers against King George III of England for cruel and inhumane treatment of those who did the work of plowing, sowing and harvesting and who received less than a living wage in return. The event was more of a massacre than a successful rebellion. Those who could leave, did so, by any means possible. Many came to America as indentured servants, paying off the bond with daily wages over a long period of time. Most of them stayed in America because it gave them opportunities of freedom and ownership of property.*

20- THE SNAKE HAZARD

Having grown up on the prairie where sharp eyes were necessary to survival, my mother knew one sound above all others—the buzz of a rattlesnake. Prairie rattlers were often small and just the color of the ground. They blended so well with their background that you often heard them before you saw them! One time, walking on the trail ahead of her and barefoot, because I loved to go barefoot in the summer, I felt my mother knock me to one side very sharply. I couldn't imagine why until she screamed at me "Rattlesnake!" I would have stepped on it with my bare foot. It was only about 20 inches long and I had not seen it! She killed the snake with a garden hoe that she carried for that purpose and did it quickly. She had had a lot of experience by that time in her life.

She told me one incident that demonstrated her ability to tell the sound of the rattlesnake from anything else. When I was about a year old, we still lived in the sod house. She had a large mirror propped against the living room wall where I could see myself and play in front of the mirror. Mama had put me there before the mirror with a doll as she prepared to go outside to do some chores. She heard that sinister buzz that only a rattlesnake can make. Grabbing me and tossing me onto a bed, she got a garden hoe and carefully tilted the mirror out from the wall. There was a fair-sized prairie rattler, coiled to strike anyone who would come close enough. He had come in through a hole made by one of the many burrowing rodents who came through the soft walls in spite of all the vigilance at trying to keep them out. Mama dispatched the rattler with her trusty garden hoe and then looked around for his mate. Snakes often go together—or so she believed. Finding none, she took the dead rattler outside and put me back in front of the mirror. After that, she always checked behind the mirror and under the furniture before leaving me alone in the house for longer than a minute or two. If she possibly could, she took me with her outside rather than risk leaving me alone.

21- THE IMPORTANCE OF FRUGALITY

As I got older, I was expected to stay in the house and "out of trouble" more and more often. I don't know how old I was at the time, but I remember that Mama would put a hatpin at a certain number on the clock. When the big hand got to that pin, I was supposed to take a big spoon and hit the bread dough in the big crockery bowl to "mix it down" so that it would rise again without getting too light. If it got "too light" it would go over the top of the crock and drip in big blobs on the cabinet top. That was bad! I had learned to tell time long before I started to school but have no idea how old I was when I was the bread-dough watcher. It was just my job and I took pride in trying to keep that dough inside the crock rather than on the cabinet or—Heaven forbid, the floor! To waste bread dough was just unforgivable.

Wasting anything was almost a sin, regardless of what it was. We lived very frugally and my parents worked terribly hard to be good providers; but nothing came easy. My mother picked sand plums that grew down along the creek about a mile away. They were large, yellow-meated plums that were very sour until just dead-ripe. She would put them on a piece of brown paper and lay them in a cool place until they all got ripe enough to eat. Then she would boil them in sugar water and pour them into glass jars while still boiling hot, putting a knife or a fork into each jar to take the first heat so that the jar wouldn't break from the hot liquid. Those plums were so good! They seemed especially good in the winter when there was no other fruit available anyplace. A few people had apple, pear and peach trees and some cherry trees. They were hard to grow but the reward was great when they got old enough to bear fruit! Mama canned almost everything she could get her hands on "for the winter." Sometimes it seemed as if we were like squirrels, storing all the food away for the winter; but winters were long and sometimes pretty severe.

It was very comforting to know that our cellar was full of good food—not just good, delicious! The walls were just earthen—no plaster, so the cellar always had an earthy smell. It stayed at about seventy degrees. That fact alone made it a wonderful place to store potatoes and apples which came in on the railroad each fall.

My mother took a special pride in having those wooden shelves along the sides of the cellar lined with glass jars full of delicious food. We would never go hungry as long as she could find food to preserve!

22- SUNDAY DINNER

As early as I can remember, we had Sunday church services at the little schoolhouse. A preacher would ride out, usually from Dodge City, spend the night and hold services the next morning. Then someone would ask him to lunch and he would ride back to Dodge in the afternoon so as to arrive before dark. I was probably four or five years old and remember well how I embarrassed my mother one Sunday.

It was our turn to invite the preacher so Mama put out a royal feed. She and her sisters were all good cooks but, of course, I thought her cooking was absolutely the finest. After the main course, Mama served some of her canned sand plums in little sauce dishes. When the preacher commented on how delicious they were, I piped up and told the man, "That's our very last jar of them, too!" Of course, Mama was mortified and turned red in the face but couldn't do much about it. My parents said I was somewhat of a "blabbermouth" before I started to school and they learned that trying to "shush" me was often worse than just letting me go ahead and "spill the beans" as they called it.

23- SCHOOL DAYS

School was the great wonderland for me because there were books we could check out and bring home to read. Both my parents had been allowed to attend school only through the fourth grade but they were avid readers and took delight in reading to me. I devoured books at a rapid rate and they became friends that kept me company while my folks were outside working—as they often were! The country school closest to our sod house was "Richland School" about three miles east—an easy ride on my pony. We usually had young teachers, not much older than some of the pupils, and I adored performing my very best for them and getting their words of praise in return. Some children didn't like school and I thought that was very strange. It was the greatest thing I could possibly imagine doing at that age. It had not occurred to me that everyone isn't attuned to learning from books and that for some it was harder to understand what was being said. I liked memory work and spelling, especially, and took great pride in bringing home my papers that had good "marks" on them. Grades were called "marks" in those days.

One cold winter day there was a very strange incident at the school. One of the children found a newborn baby in the outdoor "privy" that served for a bathroom. She didn't mention it inside the schoolhouse but told her parents on arriving home. The parents went to investigate. Sure enough, there was a lifeless little newborn down inside the "hole" beneath the seats. The parents summoned other parents who were on the school board. It was determined that the newborn probably had fallen headfirst into the pit and had not drawn a breath of life. There was only one girl old enough to produce a baby and that was the teacher, who was about fifteen at the time. The board had the delicate job of going to the home of the young teacher, Darcie, to talk with her parents. Her mother and father had been unaware that Darcie was pregnant so it was a terrible shock to them. The mother collapsed in a "faint," and Darcie began to cry, saying that it had all happened so fast. She didn't even know the baby was coming out, until kerplop! it was there. She had no idea what to do. She only knew that she had a lot of pain and that the baby had never made a sound—no crying, nothing. Darcie was allowed to stay home and another teacher was brought out from Dodge City for the remainder of the term. She married a year or two later and didn't come back to teach anymore.

24- OUR HOUSE ON THE PRAIRIE

My parents decided in 1906 to build as close to Crooked Creek as possible. The trees and a shallow water table made it more desirable than the homestead quarter a mile farther north. To my eyes, it was a two-story mansion! There were four bedrooms upstairs with gables on all sides. The south side had a portico, with doors opening onto it from both floors. The gables had some "gingerbread" but were not gaudy. There was a screened porch entry on the east and another on the west. The ground floor held a kitchen, bath, pantry, dining room, bedroom and a front parlor with a bedroom connected by an arch. The parlor was closed from the dining room by double doors. It also had a stained-glass pane above the bay window in the east. This was a big change from the sod house! Heating that much space was more than a change. It was impossible with wood and coal-burning stoves.

One bedroom over the kitchen was quite warm in winter because the brick flue went up through it from the room below. I chose to sleep there in the cold months because of the warmth.

Dad had planned waterworks that wouldn't freeze in winter. He built a well house over the windmill, connecting it to the west kitchen door of the house. Water came fresh from the well into a tank on the second floor, directly above the kitchen and bathroom. The overflow from this tank went down to a trough-tank in the well house where we stored butter, milk, cream and anything that needed to be cooled. From this tank, the overflow went to the cattle tanks out at the barn, underground. The barn was nearer the creek so the flow of water was downhill from the house. Dad believed his father-in-law's theory of putting the cold water near the house because cattle didn't care about temperature—only quantity.

For gardening in the summer, we ran a pipeful of water from the well house to the garden, making it possible to grow a lot of wonderful vegetables easily. Mama always had a big garden and canned whatever we didn't eat. Our storage cellar, near the back entrance, was full of shelves containing jars of green beans, corn, tomatoes, beef and pork, as well as sand plums, wild grape juice and currants. Dad bought potatoes and apples by the bushel whenever they came into the railroad depot at Fowler—which they did every fall. Sometimes the Rock Island agent would order salted codfish and even fresh oysters! Those were especially wonderful. My mother made big, puffy biscuits and a codfish gravy to pour over them. That was a wintertime treat without equal! Of course, her biscuits were a treat any time of year. Aunt Grace was the only person who made any biscuits to equal Mama's. They were both excellent cooks. Aunt Pearl, Uncle Walter Tullis' wife was probably just as good. Her cakes were the best I ever ate. She took such pride in each dish created as if it would be the last one ever.

I never really could understand why Aunt Grace, Aunt Pearl and my mother believed that one must set a banquet feast if anyone other than immediate family were present. It seemed to be unwritten law that must be followed almost to the point of insanity.

So I took my cue from my nearest and dearest mentors. Looking back, I wonder why it was necessary to serve duplicate sweets and, sometimes, even two meats. But that was the pattern of hospitality

I saw as I grew up. By about age forty, I had tempered my training to put out lavish meals with every welcome mat. I would sometimes have two choices of pie but I didn't serve two kinds of cake at one meal.

I honestly believe that the Tullis family's early days of deprivation led the women to try to tell the world "You'll never go hungry from my house." It's much like the child deprived of shoes. He buys too many shoes as an adult just because he can!

25- FOWLER BOOMED IN 1909

The newspaper called the <u>Gazette</u> was a great promoter of the town. It had stories about the big building boom going on. Linn Frazier was building a store that cost over $25,000. He had advertised his first store as "Dirt cheap prices in the store with the dirt floor!" It literally had a dirt floor. The new one was much grander and cleaner! That same year, W. H. Cather and William Carr built a double-front store; George Lasater and William Andis built a fancy store and the Christians and the Baptists started new church buildings!

Fremont McCauley bought fourteen lots and erected a huge machine shop to manufacture his own inventions. He really was a talented inventor of new implements and machines. He built a railroad spur to the new machine shop and set out to manufacture seriously. One thing he had invented was a *breakaway coupling* for railroad cars. Everyone who saw it agreed it was far better than any being used at that time. He made one small mistake, however. He took the coupling to the 1893 Chicago World's Fair and showed it off to several people. He had not bothered to patent the device yet. The very next year, the coupling turned up under another man's patent! As far as I know, it's still used.

Aunt Edna's husband, Frank Wilhite, and my Grandad Tullis built Fowler's first auto garage and repair shop in 1909. They called it Wilhite & Tullis and started bringing in cars from Wichita, selling them about as fast as they could bring them. One such car went to W. P. Bunyan, owner of the local hotel, who believed that autos were the wave of the future. The Fourth of July Parade was led by the town band with an automobile parade following! At that time, wheat was $1.50

per bushel and farm land $35 per acre. The <u>Gazette </u>claimed to have 750 subscribers by 1909. It had had only 275 two years before. So it was growing… The town was doing well for being only 35 years old. Prosperity seemed to be infectious and could never be wiped out—or so we thought. But we were wrong.

26- THE WAR YEARS, 1914-18

The war was looming in Europe and everyone was afraid it would spread. Farmers were encouraged by the government to plant every possible acre. It was certain there would be food shortages in Europe because of the horrible fighting there over the span of several countries. My greatest interest at that time was my mare, *Starlight*. She was a registered Morgan, dark bay with black mane and tail, with plenty of life, especially in the early mornings. For the first fifteen minutes of every morning ride, she liked walking on her hind legs. I spoiled her by letting her do it. Finally my dad put a martingale on her to keep her from the possibility of falling over backward with me. She loved to jump rails and became very good at it. I soon learned that riding astride was much safer and surer than riding sidesaddle! I could go at a full gallop and not be afraid of getting dumped if I had two feet in the stirrups. Starlight was a born prancer and loved parades. She was also a born runner and loved to exercise her talent between our place and Aunt Grace's house. We got that four miles covered pretty fast. It never occurred to me then how much faster I would be going those same miles in just a few years—in an automobile.

After Grandad Tullis got his 1918 touring car, the "car fever" really caught on in the family! The biggest excursion we ever took, during those years, was our 1918 trek to California in the touring car, camping out along the way. There were no motels and not many hotels in the West. Going down the mountains was the most exciting because the brakes would fail after getting too hot. I wish I had a picture of how we tied the trunks on the back and dragged them behind,to slow us down!

Glossary of Terms, Chapter 24-26

Martingale- *a leather collar across the horse's breast, fastened on each side to the saddle cinch, with a strap fastened to the bridle chin strap so that the horse could not lift his head high enough to fall over backward.*

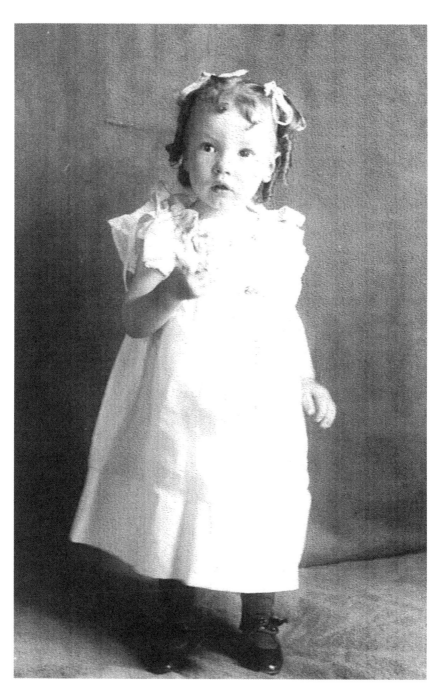

Helen McCauley Merkle. Age 16 months.

Grandmother Helen McCauley Forbes age 22.

Sod House of Will & Jessie McCauley. Built 1898/abandoned 1906.

First Grandchild of Will McCauley, Wanda Cope, age 2 in 1924.

Helen McCauley and "Capper," 1919.

Helen & Frank Cope's children, 1930. Ellen 1,
Wayne 5 and Wanda 8.

Jessie Luella Tullis, age 18 months, oldest child of Charles & Eva Tullis.

1918 California trip. McCauley's, Tullises and Spivey's.

Aunt Edna Tullis and Frank Whilhite,
wedding photo, 1900.

Helen McCauley on Starlight, spring 1919.

Aunt Belle Gilchrist, age 40.

Will & Jessie McCauley, 1912.

Kit & Billy Merkle, 1920, sons l. to r., William J., George, Charles, Carl and August.

William J. Merkle, age 3.

William J. Merkle, (1897-1983) here at age 45; married
Helen McCauley Cope. Married 41 years.

Will and Helen Merkle, ages 82 and 79.

Mary Brown McCauley, grandmother of Will. Photo 1896. Occasion: Son Charles' graduation from Kansas State College, Manhattan.

Andrew Jackson McCauley Sr. grandfather of Will. [tin type photo]

Forrest, Belle, Fremont and Charles McCauley, 1932, after Uncle Charlie's first stroke.

House that replaced the Sod House, 1906.

Steam Engine that replaced many, many horses on all the farms in the vicinity (by doing custom work for neighbors). Supposedly this was the first steam engine in the county, but I have no documentation for this statement. The owner, a great-uncle of the Sod House Baby, throught that it was the first.

27-FOURTH OF JULY

Uncle Ben's Grove became a "gathering place" for Fourth of July picnics for the people of Cave Community, Wilburn Community and even Fowler, a few miles farther south. Uncle Ben Haywood and his brother, Charley, had planted tree claims when they first came to Ford County. There were many rows of black locusts with some other kinds of trees in other rows. Several settlers planted tree claims, which had to be done to government specifications in order to have the land to plant on. Uncle Ben's claim was different because he kept it in a park-like condition that almost didn't even need a sign saying "Have your picnics here." It was a place of great beauty as well as a profitable enterprise. Trees big enough to make fence posts were very valuable!

By the time I was big enough to appreciate Uncle Ben's Grove, it had been planted about twenty-five years and had some magnificent trees, spreading their branches heavenward ,with a dense undergrowth of Sumac beneath them. Where trees had been cut for posts, new trees sprang up from the stumps; so there were trees of all sizes beneath the beautiful canopy overhead.

Uncle Ben had put a pond near the grove, at considerable cost, in which to water his cattle. However, it became a multiple-use facility! Before long, people who knew about the grove were coming there on Sundays for baptism by immersion. The first baptismal ceremony was reputed to have been held there around 1889. But the public at large saw the real charm of the place on the Fourth of July! Uncle Ben marked off a special area for ball games, another for croquet, and still another for picnic tables. It was more like a park than any city park you could imagine. His hospitality knew no bounds. He announced in the Fowler newspaper for one and all to come to the grove for the Fourth of July picnics. And come they did! It was a glorious place.

During the years of World War I, some spectacular patriotic celebrations were held. There was an "organizing committee" appointed by Uncle Ben and some of his friends. They called it "Everybody's Picnic" and they even provided transportation to and from the grove for those who lacked a way to get there! One edition of the *Fowler Gazette* referred to the crowd of nearly two thousand as being "the largest gathering ever assembled" in this vicinity. Folks came from Fowler, Meade, Minneola, Ensign, Montezuma, Dodge and even Bloom.

One year, probably 1917, there was a speaker named A.M. Harvey. He was called a "lawyer and statesman" and was running for some government office. He must not have won because I never heard of him again. Every Fourth of July saw a somewhat similar celebration with little variables. Part of the attraction was the beauty of the place. Part was the location. It was midway between Dodge City and Meade and just about midway between Minneola and Montezuma—an ideal distance for getting to the picnic and back in the same day, after the automobile came into use. Before that time, people who could be gone overnight simply planned to spend the night camping out! Those were glorious times. People got to see their neighbors and relatives and share sumptuous picnic baskets in addition to hearing fiery orators, poets and politicians and even were able to watch or participate in a ball game! You can imagine what a great day the Fourth of July was! Musicians always brought instruments so there was plenty of patriotic music. And no one could have had a better host for the event than Uncle Ben. He gloried in every minute of it, just watching all the people have a good time!

Alas, Uncle Ben departed the scene in late November of 1918, shortly after the Armistice, having a stroke at home and alone. A member of his family found him. His obituary really didn't do him justice.

Death notice of Ben Haywood as printed in _The Dodge City Globe,_ November, 1918

"B.F. Haywood, Old Settler, dies" was the headline. The piece went on to say, *"One-time driver of P.G. Reynolds' Stage Coach here was a victim of paralysis Saturday."* (Doctors thought then that "paralysis" was a *diagnosis* rather than a sign of something going on inside the head or in the nervous system.)

> *"Ben F. Haywood, Ford county resident since 1879 and former coach driver for P. G. Reynolds, Sr., in the early days of Dodge City, died at his home in Wilburn township Saturday night of paralysis. Mr. Haywood was about 70 years of age. He came here from Alpena, Michigan, in the late seventies and has lived here continuously since that time. His birthplace was Maine. A brother, Charles Haywood lives in Fowler where burial will probably be...*

"Mr. Haywood will be remembered by a number of older residents here. After a number of years in service as stage driver, he removed to a farm in southern Ford County. By his industry, he developed his farm into one of the best in the country and also accumulated other property. He was reported to be worth about $75,000."

Describing Uncle Ben by his financial worth hardly did justice to such a man! He was a poet, a philosopher, a soil scientist and an all around wonderful man who saw good in people, even when it was hard to find! I felt sorry for the writer of that piece. He had never *known* Uncle Ben so I could feel very sorry for him.

Since Ben died without a will, his farm went in thirds to his brother Charley, sister Nettie Boynton, and to the two sons of his older brother John, who had died earlier. John's two sons, Herbie and Ernie, were anything but farmers. Because they had already failed at everything else they had attempted, they came out to Ford County to occupy Uncle Ben's house and farm. It was disaster for everyone. They got into a quarrel with a neighbor, supposedly over a fence line. Angry words followed and the brothers got arrested for beating the neighbor severely. As all this occurred in the middle of June—harvest time, the trial for the two brothers was postponed to September. Both were "convicted" of battery and were fined about $200 and court costs. Eventually they left the neighborhood and the county. Uncle Ben's grove went to ruin in the twenties. Because there was no one to take care of it and keep it in that elegant condition of which Uncle Ben was so proud—simply no one to do that much hard work, it died a natural death as a park and a meeting place for the surrounding communities. It was the end of an era. The Old Settlers' Picnics were held in Dodge City and Meade for awhile and in a few other communities, but they were just not the lively kind of celebrations that had taken place in Uncle Ben's Grove!

28- END OF WORLD WAR I

When the Armistice of World War I was signed on November 11, 1918, that was to be the end of all wars. Woodrow Wilson was President and had the idea that a *League of Nations,* which was forming in Europe, was going to be the great answer for settling disputes among all countries of the world. There was a lot of talk in the newspapers about its being a great organization but Wilson wasn't able to sell the Congress on the idea and our country never joined.

As men came home from their military service, they were interested in taking up their lives where they had left off and in getting married and establishing homes. That was how I met your father. His parents, Henry and Buna Cope, had bought a place about a mile east of us during the war and Harry, his younger brother, had stayed home from the military to run the farm. Frank had been in college at Manhattan at the time. It was called *Kansas State College of Agriculture and Applied Science* then.

At the end of his junior year, Frank joined the army and was stationed in Texas. He advanced rapidly and spent the rest of his military time training troops. With the signing of the Armistice, the thousands of troops in training were let go rapidly. It was after he returned home that we met and courted. We were married in September, 1921. I was Mrs. Frank Cope—"career" enough for any small town girl. Or so I thought at the time…

My parents had not let me finish high school during the war because it was pretty hard to find the money. They didn't want me to live in town during the week---that was costly. Mostly, they didn't want their only child to be away from them—especially since it gave her ideas about wanting to go on to higher study or to nurse's training! I resented the clinging but tolerated it because there was plenty going on in my life. I had beaus and many social activities. I did not realize until more than ten years later how their decision would influence my life. There was no law that said I had to go to high school, so I simply stayed home in what would have been my third year. I was ignorant and blissful!

29-HOW THE ROARING TWENTIES ROARED

By the mid-1920's, Fowler was a little beehive of business activity on the prairie. Located on U.S. Highway 54, it had a thriving Chicago, Rock Island and Pacific Railway station. There was a 24-inch artesian well that pumped into a 70,000-gallon storage tank. Electric service from the Kansas Power Company's Dodge City plant supplied electricity 24 hours daily.

There were four churches, Catholic, Methodist, Friends and Christian and a Class "A" high school and grade school. The old Friends Academy had closed when the high school was built. Businesses included three general merchandise stores, three dry goods stores, two hardware, lumber yard, meat market, newspaper, drug store, two banks, dry cleaner, doctor, two barber shops, four cream stations, three garages, modern hotel, theatre, four grain elevators, two dentists, two gasoline stations, and good telephone service. In addition, there were service clubs and lodges of several national groups and the Fowler Community Club boasted 175 members! If you add in all the insurance companies, painters, carpenters and other service people, you can see that we thought we were on top of the world. There was even a municipal band whose members gave concerts every Friday evening. By 1928, there was both a junior and a senior band totaling well over fifty people. The band was financed by a one-half mill levy on the city and township. The open-air concerts in the summer were a big drawing card to bring people to Fowler. Certain stores kept longer hours on Fridays to accommodate customers. By anyone's standards, it was a thriving town and agriculture was its backbone. The local elevators were buying wheat for $1.70 per bushel. The local editor of *Fowler News* claimed that one million, three hundred thousand bushels of wheat were raised in the Fowler trade area in 1926 and 1928 was an even bigger year!

By June, 1922, I had my firstborn, Wanda, a beautiful baby if I ever saw one. Your father had gone into business as an automobile dealer in Fowler and I became a young matron with a happy home life and busy social life. I was already a member of the Women's Auxiliary, the Methodist Ladies' Circle, the Red Cross and a couple other "Societies." Add to that a baby and I was very busy. In June, 1925, my second child was a boy, Wayne—almost ten pounds, which was any grandfather's delight—mostly because they had wanted a boy. Two children were more than a handful for me and I was thankful when my parents moved to Fowler –for obvious reasons. My mother was probably the most maternal human being who ever lived. She instantly "took over" the spoiling of the children. If she was a little faint-hearted in the fall of '28 when I told her I was going to deliver again, she didn't show it! In June, 1929, my second daughter and third child, Ellen, was born.

To be perfectly frank, she wasn't much to look at! The cord had been wrapped around her neck and she was very blue and lifeless-looking. Dr. Robb had torn himself away from one of his baseball games to come to the house and "take a look," in his casual manner. By the time he got in the door, the actual birth was already over. He took one glance and put the baby over on the top of the dresser. There was no cry—nothing coming from the baby. My mother was greatly disturbed by that. She grabbed the baby, turned her upside down, got some sounds out as well as some mucous and finally—a good, loud cry. She immersed the scrawny, blue body into a pan full of warm water. That seemed to do the trick. There was wailing and flailing of limbs as the anything-but-beautiful little creature caught onto life. Blue gradually turned pink as she got more air into her lungs.

The other two babies were breast-fed and seemed to thrive from the beginning of life. The third one was different. Nothing agreed with her. She was always hungry, always vomiting and always fussy—your typical "colicky baby." After three months of being up "all night every night," I heard of a vacuum-packed powder called "Nestle's Food" and decided "why not?" Nothing else had worked. We had already been through cow's milk and goat's milk and were beginning to feel desperate. After a few days on Nestles Food, I had a happy baby at last! She began to keep her food down and the colic disappeared. She slept through the night within a few hours of the first feeding of the new food. I was so thankful. Within a few months she was fat and happy. No one can know the relief I felt after a three-month battle with a colicky baby who threw up at the slightest provocation. No one knew much about allergies in those days. How could a baby be allergic to milk? It sounded impossible but believe me, she was!

Prior to 1929, we had bought farmland in southeast Colorado, Baca County to be exact. Frank would go out there to do his plowing and planting and I would go along, leaving the baby with my mother after her diet problems were solved. The Colorado "vacation" was anything *but*. It was more like a nightmare. We stayed in a dilapidated farmhouse—abandoned by previous dwellers—a house with no conveniences and many unseen occupants—mostly mice. Outside was a much worse hazard— rattlesnakes galore. Wayne was four that summer and had a tendency to "go see Daddy" even though Daddy was a mile or more away—across a rattlesnake-infested field. In spite of all my diligence, he would disappear and I would start looking and calling. I was horrified one time, seeing him go "zigzag" across a pasture—the best short-cut to the field, except for the rattlesnakes. I found out, as I followed him, that he was "zigzagging" each time he would hear a rattler buzz a warning. That pasture seemed to be a whole den full of snakes, all of them buzzing their warnings. I soon found myself "zigzagging" to go around the snakes. I had to keep going because the child was still ahead of me, making good time, and I couldn't go back without him! I had learned my lesson.

There would be no more Colorado trips for me. I did go a few times after that but my parents kept the children. The hot, dusty fields of Eastern Colorado, the severe thunderstorms, the rattlesnakes, the difficult journey to and from Pritchett, the nearest town where supplies could be bought—all were history for me within a few years.

27- THE DESPERATE, DIRTY THIRTIES

In September, 1933, Frank came home sick after farming in Colorado for two weeks. He had along another man helping him. His being too sick to drive indicated to me he was pretty bad. He always liked to be the driver and the person in charge. He had a fever and stiff, painful neck. Within one week he was paralyzed—and could no longer stand up. Two of our employees from the Chevrolet Agency helped take him to Dodge City. He resisted, not wanting to run up a hospital bill on top of our other debts. Grabbing hold of the bedpost with his right hand—the only one that was usable, he tried to keep from going. He knew that Colorado was rife with "sleeping sickness" and that he had been bitten by hundreds of mosquitoes over the past month. He had already put the picture together in his own mind and knew that he had the same sleeping sickness that was killing horses in Colorado.

Within two weeks from becoming sick, shortly after we removed him to St.Anthony's Hospital in Dodge City, he died. The town's leading Internist , Dr. Dennis, said it was Encephalitis, also called "sleeping sickness." That disease had been raging throughout the southwestern states. All the mosquito bites he had received out in the Colorado fields had been the contributors!

To describe me as "devastated" would not be adequate. I felt destroyed—completely. I went through all the stages of disbelief, denial, resentment, anger and a consuming grief, one by one and sometimes all at the same time. Why me, Lord? Because that's the way life is. It rains on the just and the unjust. I had been rained on terribly, in my opinion. I didn't really think God had singled me out for special punishment. I was just hurt to the very core that my life had suddenly shattered into a thousand pieces. It finally sank in on me: this was no longer the roaring twenties we had enjoyed. This was the dreadful, dirty thirties; we were in the midst of a horrible depression; I had a mountain of debts and three children to support! I had no income and no qualifications for earning any. I was not capable of planning a funeral for my husband. My numbness made me rely on the strength of others—my parents, my friends and some relatives. Lena and Alice Johnson, the wives of Egbert and Albert, our two mechanics, were pillars of strength. They took over the children and saw them through the funeral. They decided the Friends Church would be the only one large enough to hold the crowd. Being a business owner on Main Street, Frank knew hundreds of people on a first-name basis. He was an extraordinary extrovert who never forgot a name or a face. People I didn't recognize came from afar. My two older children, crushed, understood that "death" meant "not coming back." My youngest, curious, kept asking when her daddy was going to wake up! I found myself wishing I could be like the baby and believe that he was just asleep and would waken soon. Words and tune of a hymn sung that day stayed with me for years. *"Out of the Ivory Palaces, into a world of woe..."* I identified with *"world of woe."* Rain had seemingly ceased over the high plains. The winds became constant, sifting the dry loose topsoil back and forth week after week and wore on into months. It was never-ending!

31- BACK TO THE FARM

Had it not been for my parents, I have no idea what I would have done in my desperate situation. Debts at the garage were just not collectible. The few who had money would walk across the street to avoid meeting me. Sending out bills was a hopeless gesture. I owed more at the car agency than I had on deposit in the bank! My dad and our lawyer, C. C. Wilson, finally worked out a plan for me to give the garage and equipment to Egbert and Albert Johnson, our two full-time mechanics, in return for back wages and a new, 1934 Chevy sedan they hadn't been able to sell. They assumed the accounts payable that I couldn't pay and became the new owners. I had a difficult time "forgiving" the debtors who turned up occasionally with new cars or trucks from a neighboring dealer, since they "didn't have the money" to pay their debts to me. That was Lesson Number One of many to follow.

My parents thought we would be better off living with them in the country where we would all live together in the two-story, five bedroom house, have room to garden and raise our food. Of course they were right. They suddenly had six mouths to feed instead of two! The fact that I had no higher education came home to haunt me pretty fast. I probably couldn't have found a job, even with two college degrees; but in truth, I wasn't qualified to do any kind of work for remuneration— except scrub floors. And there was a terrible over-supply of floor scrubbers.

Going back to the house I had lived in from 1906 to 1921 seemed like a dream that was happening to someone else. I couldn't believe it but it was real. I just wasn't ready to acknowledge that I was starting life over at age thirty-three.

The pathetic little dab of furniture worth saving was fitted into the parlor and front bedroom at the farm. The rest was left for the new tenants. I was able to rent the house to a local carpenter for $8 per month. My parents rented their two-story, four-bedroom house across the same block for $12 monthly! Such were the prices in Fowler in 1934. We were fortunate to be able to find people who could actually pay the rent and take care of the property responsibly. At that time, Fowler still had four churches two groceries, two barbers, two restaurants, two car agencies, a lumber yard-hardware, a grain elevator, a blacksmith shop, two farm machinery dealers, a mortuary and furniture store, a bank—the other having closed in the bank "holiday" of 1931.

Frankie Bergkamp's restaurant served a huge hamburger for five cents and a generous milkshake—two tall glasses full, for ten cents. Wheat delivered to the elevator, brought twenty-five cents per bushel. Baby calves and pigs sometimes could not be sold at all because there were no buyers! Most herds of cattle on the farms existed on tumbleweeds and wheat straw, when it could be found. The drought just seemed to go on and on and on.

In 1932, Franklin D. Roosevelt, known as FDR, was elected President. He was going to save the country with a lot of Public Works Programs. Men could get a "job" with Civilian Conservation Corps, CCC, or with the Works Progress Administration, WPA, to build public buildings or roads. The work was run like most government things, with poor efficiency, but at least people could have some kind of job that paid. It was really the onset of World War II that bailed out FDR's government program. However, poor as they were, the public work programs were better than having no job at all. They gave people a reason to get up in the mornings and go to work!

We had good schools and well-qualified teachers. It was a blessing to know that I could send the two older children on the bus in the morning and know they would return in the evening a little smarter than when they had gone out the door. Mama always had an admonition for me when I was little. On going out the door, she would give me a kiss and say "Now try to act smarter than you are!" I found myself doing the same thing to Wanda and Wayne!

There was no grief "counseling" in those days and everyone who lost a loved one just had to jump in and start swimming upstream. You made the best of what you had—whether you had much or not. I was ill-equipped to be both a mother and a father but that was the role I had inherited!

One sympathetic soul came up to me during my time of grief and told me she knew just how I felt because she had lost her father. I wanted to say, "You can't possibly know how I feel..." but thought better of it. Something told me she meant well. It was just a poor comparison! I learned never to be surprised at what people will say!

32- DOOR-TO-DOOR SELLING

My friends, Vern and Opal Adams, in Montezuma, invited me to their "company party" about 1935. They were selling magazines for *Successful Farming* publishers and thought I should try that to make a living. It certainly was a learning experience but not very rewarding financially. The "market" for the magazine was principally destitute farmers who had no cash to pay for anything of necessity, much less a magazine subscription. People wanted to pay with chickens, eggs, vegetables or some other produce; but the company wanted cash. My career at selling was pretty short. It didn't take long to conclude that I wasn't earning anything more than my gasoline, much less the wear and tear on my car! I had to give up the sales career. It got me out of the house among people; however, it was anything but fruitful.

Western Kansas was battered by terrible, persistent winds in the mid-thirties. Much has been written about the "black Sunday," that came on Palm Sunday, 1935. It was hard to describe. The day dawned beautiful and remained calm until right after lunch. Someone looked out a north window and saw boiling, black dirt swirling in very suddenly and fiercely. Day changed to night in a matter of minutes. We had to light lanterns to see inside the house! My mother and I went outside to try to retrieve some of her hens that had flocks of baby chickens. Fortunately, the hens sat down and spread their wings because of the darkness, enabling the chicks to get under them— otherwise they would have blown away. Grandad Tullis had eaten Sunday dinner with us. As a widower, he lived one mile north with

Uncle Wiley. He made the instant decision to head for home! He was in his eighties and frail.

My dad didn't want him to go out in such a storm but he was not to be deterred by anyone! After about a half-hour, my dad announced that he would go see if Grandad had made it back home. That drew a protest from my mother but she knew he would do what he thought best. Dad tied a tea towel around his face to keep out the dirt and put on a visor cap to hold it in place. He lighted a kerosene lantern and headed out to the north, walking one mile clinging to a barbed-wire fence because he knew it led to Wiley's place. He came back in less than two hours. Grandad had gotten safely home.

I felt blest to have three children who were bright enough to learn when given the opportunity. I resolved to give them as many opportunities as I could afford. With that resolve, we purchased two violins and an old upright piano...

The hard part came with trying to get the little musicians to practice! My admonitions on practice drew everything from limp indifference to bristling resentment, depending on what other attraction was at hand for them to "miss." We endured for two years in which time we mastered "Abide With Me" – a very melancholy version of it—and two other hymns. We didn't get as far as "Humoresque." I had met my match. The children won round one. I determined that the youngest child would learn to play the piano. She was beginning to hang around the piano and try a few little ditties on her own. I started her on lessons at age five. I tried to console myself that one out of three wasn't too bad for an average. Piano lessons cost fifty cents for one hour. Teachers were thrilled to get a student who would practice and never shorted on that hour. The community was blest with several gifted musicians who gave lessons. Competition probably helped keep the price low. Lessons didn't go up to one dollar until about 1941. By then, everything was rising in price because of World War II.

I learned to sew out of necessity, making all the clothing for both girls up through 1941. Louise Norman Cope, who had divorced from Harry, my brother-in-law, had an aunt, Mary Wood, whose husband was fairly prosperous. She gave Louise bundles of her daughter Hazel's *hand-me-downs*. From those, I was able to clothe both my daughters quite well. They were always proud to wear the things I made and praised me for my efforts. Neither girl had a ready-made coat until about 1941. Then the wool garments were made of re-used wool because all new wool went to military uniforms. Most wool was "tweed" because of the quality of yarns available. No one ever complained. The war effort came first. Most people were glad to make the sacrifices of not having high quality woolens—not to mention gasoline, sugar, coffee and some other things in short supply. There was very little "hoarding" of any scarce commodity, at least in our community.There were some stories of black markets going on in some of the cities—of scarce commodities being diverted to markets that drew premium prices. Since the radio news dealt mostly with events of the war, we didn't get a lot of news about anything as mundane as people hoarding scarce items. Occasionally the news- papers carried stories about people trying to profiteer off the war and off things that were in short supply.

Louise and her three little Copes lived with her mother, Julia Norman, in the Artesian Valley. Her two brothers, Howard and Bill, were still unmarried and at home at that time. They helped Louise's children, George, Norma and Dorothy, to develop a sense of identity and to feel loved. Since they were both musicians, the three children got to sing a lot. The girls learned to play piano quite well. After George graduated from high school, Louise married Loren Beach, and the entire family moved to California in 1941. Norma and Dorothy finished high school there.

George served in the military during WWII and went to college afterward. He married a woman named Madelyn, had two daughters, Wendy and Tanya, and was killed in a car wreck on a California highway, along with his mother, Louise, and her husband, Loren, about 1954. Norma married Russell Wiitala and they had a son, Russell, and two daughters, Sonja and Teresa. Dorothy married Durand Cole and had two daughters, Julie and Georgette. They settled in Washington State and remained there.

I was very fond of Louise and her children. In spite of economic woes, we had many good times together during the thirties and remained loyal friends up until her death. I was fond of the whole Norman family. They treated me like family and filled a very important spot in my life during those trying years.

I'm not sure who made the suggestion, but someone in 1937 thought it would be a good idea to raise turkeys. The whole countryside was overrun with grasshoppers—millions of them. It was logical that the turkeys could live on a diet of grasshoppers. After all, the insects were a source of protein! My three children loved to be outdoors. They could take the turkeys from place to place to pursue the grasshoppers— or so I thought. It didn't work out quite as I had imagined but it was the source for some funny stories later. The few we ate were delicious.

Turkeys, I found, didn't really have any instinct for staying in a flock or moving from place to place in a group. They were about as easy to "herd" as cats would have been. They had a talent for straying apart from the group, getting lost in tall weeds, becoming terribly frightened over "nothing" and taking off in the wrong direction with wings flapping. Turkeys didn't hunt grasshoppers as a group, but as individuals! They would go first one direction, then another, without any kind of "togetherness."

We soon learned to turn the turkeys out only in the cool of the morning and to put them back in their shelter in the heat of the day. They could fly over fences, landing high up in trees. When they began to get their fill of grasshoppers, they were even more un-cooperative! My children rejoiced when the turkeys got big enough to go to market. They had learned more about turkeys than they ever wanted to know. It was pretty much a learning experience, for the price of turkeys was terrible that fall—just like the price of everything else. We did enjoy their tasty meat at Thanksgiving and Christmas and were thankful to be able to share them with some of our relatives!

One bright spot in the summer of 1936 was the new baby in the neighborhood. Earnest and Ethel Lee who worked for Uncle Fremont, decided to adopt a baby boy who was born locally. Lee's were good people and Uncle Fremont expected both of them to work for what amounted to slave wages. Being the miser that he was, he had not improved his house to include any conveniences. Ethel was still cooking on a wood-burning range and her kitchen was anything but convenient. She was expected to serve three meals every day to several hired hands. Fremont called on me to come help her through harvest. I was to receive $1 per day and my meals. That was the height of generosity for Fremont. Since I lived only 2 ½ miles away, I could stay home at night.

I helped Ethel get Donald started in life. He was a good baby and it was pretty obvious he had fallen into a loving home! I had never really lived in a house with Uncle Fremont before, taking care to avoid him at family gatherings when possible, because I found his dourness unpleasant. However, he had a funny side to his nature that surfaced on occasion. Some of his habits were eccentric, in my opinion, and his explosive temper was something to behold.

One afternoon, two young men went back to the field to run the tractor and combine, both of which needed drivers. There were no self-propelled machines at that time. Daniel Hanna and John Frazier had just graduated from high school. They were happy-go-lucky and prone to have a good time in any situation. Somehow, they failed to notice that the combine was too wide to pass between two trees standing out in the wheat field. Daniel was the tractor driver and tried to take the narrow path, regardless; John was yelling at the top of his voice for Daniel to stop but Daniel never looked back. The grain tank was the tallest thing on the machine. It was ripped off and badly bent. Wheat harvest came to a halt that day! Uncle Fremont was "fit to be tied." I had never seen him so mad. The men who worked around him all the time said that was pretty typical of him. I know my dad didn't like to work for him and avoided doing so whenever he could. He always treated him with respect but never with any warmth or affection.

Dad liked Earnest Lee and they had an affection for each other. He would help Earnest in any way he could and sometimes did. I was fond of Ethel from our first meeting. She was a genuinely good woman and tried to live her beliefs. I know she didn't have an easy time pleasing Uncle Fremont. I'm sure he tried to make her life as difficult as possible—as he seemed to do to all those around him. I went back in November, 1938, and helped Ethel with their new son, Richard, born to them almost three years after they had adopted Donald. She was more relaxed taking care of him and seemed to do well. Part of the difference, I am sure, was that Uncle Fremont was no longer around. He had passed on to his reward—whatever it was—a year earlier.

33- WORLD WAR II YEARS, 1941-45

By the time 1940 rolled around, it was generally understood by Americans that our country was headed for war in Europe; it was just a question of *when*. Adolph Hitler was making impossible demands on England. At first Neville Chamberlain tried to make peace by giving in to the demands. That proved to be hopeless. There was a joke going around that Hitler wanted PEACE—"a piece of Poland, a piece of Hungary and a piece of Czechoslovakia." All the average citizen knew was what he read in the newspapers—as Will Rogers used to say. So I suppose the government "fed" us what they wanted us to know. The newspapers were full of war rumors; radio emphasized the same rumors; the newsreels at the movie houses gave the same stories—only much more graphic details. Some of the pictures were of terrible and bloody events. Every evening my dad would tune in on the battery radio for the news from Europe. Those were tense, terrible months in late 1940 and most of 1941.

I knew that I needed to get a job that paid at least some of my expenses. I felt so terrible about my parents' having to bear all the cost of my children's expenses. One day when I was in the bank, I asked Maggie Morrison what she thought I should do—where she would advise me to look for a job. She looked at me with that straightforward gaze that only she could cast and said, "Do you want a housekeeping job?" I answered that I would take just about anything. I just needed some money coming in so desperately. She told me that one of her clients was looking for a housekeeper and that he was a very kind and decent gentleman. I wouldn't have to worry about his character or any untoward intentions. I told her I wouldn't go anyplace as a live-in housekeeper unless I could take my youngest child because I didn't want to put all the burden of three children on my mother. She gave me the man's name and telephone number and I called him the next day for an interview. He told me to come over for a talk and I went. That was how I met the most pleasant man I had ever seen! He just radiated goodness. He said that bringing a child along would not be a problem for him and added with a twinkle in his eye, "She probably won't eat a whole lot, anyway."

The wages would be $1 per day plus board and room for mother and child. He would prefer I work six days per week but I could have a day off now and then if needed. I would do all the housekeeping, including meals for one hired man who lived there. I would also do the man's laundry because he had no place to do it. He was usually gone on Saturday nights and Sundays. As it turned out, the hired man, Jess, often didn't make it back on Mondays, because of his imbibing habits; but I didn't know that at the time. I was just tickled to death to have a job!

As I learned during my interview, the elderly father had died in February of that year and as the spring work came on, the farm work plus the cooking and laundry presented an overwhelming amount of work. Bear in mind that in 1941, people were still using horses and mules to pull their feed wagons while they fed cattle. The elderly father had done the cooking and the laundry almost up until his death but had been unable to keep the house up. Things had "gotten behind" a little!

The house was "modern" in that it had hot and cold running water and a bathroom inside. Electricity was provided by a 32 volt "Windcharger" that had batteries in the nearby fruit cellar. The batteries were direct current—DC –so all the appliances that ran off them had to be DC also. The ceiling lights and electric iron were about all that the system could supply! The kitchen contained a huge wood-burning range with a water tank on one side, plus a gas range of about 1929 vintage. It ran on butane gas from a 100lb. gas "bottle." There were no new appliances available at that time because the war effort was in full swing and all the U.S. factories had geared up to make tanks, guns and other war items. The fridge was a real antique, somewhat unreliable, and had a two-door icebox nearby that was the backup. Some floors were covered with a linoleum and the bedrooms had bare, tongue-and-grooved, boards, without any sub-floor beneath.

The house had been two old houses moved to the farm in 1896 after the first two years in a sod house. It was all that a German immigrant thought he could afford at the time. He had brought it across the buffalo grass pastures from the burned-out town of Montezuma, with a twelve-mule team. There were no roads at that time—only trails. Six of the couple's seven children had been born in that house *before* it had running water or a bathroom! The first child, Matilda, had been born in the "three room sod mansion" the couple had occupied until 1896.

So that was how I met Will Merkle, son of a German stowaway who had left his native home in order to avoid the Kaiser's military service, coming to Kansas after disenchantment with immigrant life in

Illinois, apprenticed to a baker at age fifteen. Will was the second child—Matilda , or Tillie as she was known, being the oldest. They were followed by Grace, about my age, then George, Charles, Carl and Augustus in that order.

After I had worked as a housekeeper on the farm for about a year, one day, out of the blue, I received a proposal of marriage. The rest is—as they say, history. I accepted the idea of marriage whole-heartedly. I knew I would never, ever meet anyone kinder or nicer or more full of fun than Will Merkle. He was a unique person and certainly one of the most agreeable men on the face of the earth. I had dated several men during my eight years of widowhood. Believe me, none of them measured up to my standards of what a husband should be! The most amazing thing to me was that Will just accepted my children as if they were "part of the package." It probably helped that the two older ones were sixteen and nineteen; they wouldn't be around very long. He had such a spirit of generosity with both them and my parents—to whom I was still the "only child!" They accepted Will as being the nicest man they had ever met—which I'm sure he was. He was always polite and pleasant; his twinkling blue eyes were his defining feature. In a room full of strangers meeting for the first time, he would be referred to as the man with the smiling blue eyes.

We laughed about it many times that first year I was here that we had been born only nine miles apart and grown up literally seven miles distant from each other without our ever being acquainted! Actually we had met one time when we were teen-agers at a housewarming in the Cliff Wetmore home. It was about 1912 so I would have been about thirteen and Will about sixteen. We were both shy and awkward; so it wasn't a very memorable meeting. He wasn't allowed to go to high school; instead his father worked him from dawn to dusk, just like his family before him had had to work in Germany! At age twenty-one, Will had been drafted into the Army and sent to Camp Funston in Kansas. The Armistice was signed in November, 1918; so he never went beyond the state boundaries.

Seven miles was a lot farther distant in those days than it is now—so we just never had occasion to get together. How strange life is—that we could be that close in distance but not know each other until we were in our forties! I had never thought much about the doctrine of pre-destination until I reflected upon how we two had grown up in such proximity but had not had any social contact with each other until mid-life!

I think Will had always had to work terribly hard. His father had lost his grip on the others when they married so he kept an even firmer grip on his firstborn son! He always had to harness the workhorses about 4:30 in the morning, returning to the house to eat breakfast before 7 a.m. He chopped all the wood for his aged parents and did all the "hard jobs" that he could to make their lives better. He told me that the only trip he got to take was to Pikes Peak, Colorado, in 1929 when August graduated from high school. His mother had promised the trip for graduation and took her eldest son as well as her baby.

August went to Kansas State but never graduated. He spent $4,000 his first year—a staggering sum for 1929-30. Then his father told him he'd better learn how to earn money instead of spending it. One thing he did for his mother was to install plumbing in the bathroom and kitchen. The water pipes looked as if they were made mostly of "fittings" and were almost comical to see but they did work. All those years of carrying water and heating bath water on a stove were finally ended. The poor lady died in 1937 so she didn't get to enjoy August's master plumbing job very long.

August had a very pleasant personality and loved to socialize. He went out of his way to make sure that I knew he was glad for his brother to have a wife "to look after him." Will's two sisters, Tillie and Grace also made a special point of telling me they were so glad Will had found a wife who would love him and take care of him. They were sincere and I appreciated their welcoming honesty. They loved their brother and had been worried that he would "just be a hermit" after the parents were gone.

Carl and Phronie were friendly to me from the time I came here to live. Carl, next youngest, loved to eat at his old home table, a large, square, oak pedestal style that occupied the center of the kitchen. He was probably the most gregarious of all the brothers and made no bones about how glad he was to be back at the old home kitchen. He and Phronie were both very plain-spoken. No one had to doubt where they stood on any issue. I liked that about both of them.

On the December day that Phronie went into labor with Sharon, she and Carl stopped by to tell us they were enroute to Dodge City to the hospital. She thought it would be a short labor. Dr. Daugherty, her attending physician, examined her before they came by here and told her he thought it would be a long labor. She related to me later that evening that he appeared at her hospital room about 6 p.m. with a book in hand that he was planning to read while she continued her labor. He asked her how she was feeling. She told him she was feeling "not exactly wonderful, but I do feel a lot better since the baby came." He was pretty slack-jawed over that. He had not bothered to stop by the nursing station and read her chart. Another doctor had had to deliver Sharon Sue! Phronie never let Dr. Daugherty forget his error in judgement. She was a good nurse and usually knew what she was talking about. We saw Charlie and Hazel much less than Carl and Phronie because there was so much distance between us. They lived twenty miles southeast of Meade, where the only gates were cattle-guards to keep herds separate from each other. I can truthfully say that they were always cordial to me and a hundred percent supportive. Charlie was the marathon talker in the family. Will used to say "He took after Uncle Jake." (Wolfely, his mother's brother.) I never had the privilege of meeting Uncle Jake so had to take his word for it. He did talk twice as fast as the rest of the brothers and got twice as much said. Some of his tales were pretty interesting and had some elements of doubt in them. But dull they were not! George and Edna lived only a mile west of us but were not enthusiastic about my entry into the family. After about ten years, they decided I was here to stay and mellowed a great deal. Poor George developed a medical problem, Alzheimer's probably—and spent his last seven years in a nursing home. Edna went faithfully every day to feed him. It was a lonely vigil. He didn't even recognize her when she was in the room.

I was always amazed at how much Will knew of history, math and geography—especially for one who had not gone beyond eighth grade. It was a pity he had not had the opportunity to go to college that August had! An eighth grade graduate in those days was much different from one in modern times! Courses were pretty demanding. In the country schools, a student could progress at his own speed if he happened to be the only one in the class. I think some of the country schools were better than some of the consolidated districts. Teachers were held to pretty high standards, too.

That was one reason I didn't hesitate to take my youngest child out of the Fowler school in sixth grade and move her to the Pleasant View district just two miles from the Merkle farm. The teacher was a wonderful woman, named Rachel Crown; she probably was the most dedicated and thorough teacher in the county! Unfortunately that lasted only two terms. She decided to go back to college for further study.

Her dad was the Cave Church preacher southwest of Ensign. She lived at home and drove over to Pleasant View, a distance of twelve or thirteen miles, one way. There were several Crown children. I don't know if they were all as intelligent and dedicated as their older sister—probably not. I always regretted not getting to go on to higher education but have no way of knowing whether I would have succeeded. Because I had been kept at home, I determined to give my children the opportunity to study if they wanted it. At least I would lead the horse to water; if he didn't drink, it wouldn't be my fault…That is how any parent has to look at the things he cannot change.

34- ABANDONED FARMSTEADS IN THE COUNTRYSIDE

A drive through the country nowadays is mostly just a drive past old windmills, old crumbled foundations surrounded by a few lilac bushes, a cedar tree or two and—in a wet year, clusters of the lovely old Larkspur, a perennial flower as hardy as the people who planted it!

Nothing is any sadder than to look at all the abandoned farmsteads in all directions from Crooked Creek and in the Valley! It used to be a community so "alive with people" and now it's just an empty shadow.

From the Meade – Gray County Line, you could go north a mile to what was Art Dodson's beautiful home built about 1929. In any direction from that you could see beautiful farms with windmills, trees, barns and corrals. They're gone—absorbed by absentee owners buying them from heirs who couldn't make a go of it for whatever reason, mostly not enough acres to merit their investment in high-priced machinery!

The Wetmores, Wrights, Lattas and Conrads are gone from their homesteads. Farther east, the Tullis land all has other names on it. Only one house remains, Grandad's. Uncle Walter occupied it when he married Aunt Pearl (Gamble) and then enlarged it in 1935 to a two-story frame with hardwood floors and lots of closets under the eaves. They lived there until 1955 when Aunt Pearl took her own life. She had been suffering from depression but no one realized how severe it was. That was a devastating blow for Uncle Walter and for all of us. Onis and Thurman Eccleston lived there quite a while after that and later their daughter, Charlotte Morrison. Uncle Wiley's place is long gone. Also my parents' place. It burned to the ground and all the granaries and outbuildings just sat there and rotted. I could barely endure going over there! Uncle Forrest's and my cousin, Andrew's homes were leveled when the man from Dodge City got title to it in the early forties. Uncle Charley's house burned in 1936. The new house on the same farmstead, built in the late 20's, still stands and has been greatly remodeled and improved. Uncle Fremont's house was built of some kind of concrete block. Ernest Lee's grandson restored it. The old shop where Fremont did most of his work was let fall down. It was too near the creek and was all wood. The Lee's built more fireproof buildings.

On down the creek, the Haywood landscape is a shadow of its former glory. The Bunyan place changed.for the worse. My friend, Rosetta Bunyan, Harvey Way's mother, once lived in that neighborhood. Hers was a sad, sad story.

In the Artesian Valley, the big turn-of-the-century houses are about all gone. Frank Sourbier's six miles west of Fowler, was one of the earliest of the early farmsteads. Nellie Sourbier grew up there. She married Robert Brannan, had four sons, Fenton, Frank, Charles , Raymond "Pat", and daughter Betty. In 1906 the Sourbier home was sold. Jim Turner lived there most of my adult life. It's empty now but still there! The thing that really marks the site is the huge Cottonwood tree still standing over the one-story house, one of the first frame homes in the valley. Every fall, when its leaves change, it's a striking, memorable sight.

Sourbiers had six children. I don't know what became of all of them; but their oldest son, Charles K., had polio before they came from Pennsylvania in 1879. The parents were advised to "go west" for his health. He became Meade's first jeweler and clock repairman and was well known for his honesty and industriousness. His store was on the north side of the main street, West Carthage, in the first block, next door to where the Brannan Brothers had their International machinery agency so long. Charles Sourbier died in 1940. The youngest Sourbier child, Anna Griggs, lived to a ripe old age in Meade. That jewelry and clock shop was one of the longest lasting businesses in Meade just west of the Lakeway Hotel.

The Lakeway was built in 1929 by a stock company formed in 1926. It was first operated by S.D. and Belle Adams and daughter, Alice. The fireproof walls and floors made it distinctly "modern." The coffee shop, run by Alice, was "the place to eat!" Most impressive to me was the lobby, furnished in green leather sofas and chairs in front of a big fireplace on the west wall. A wide stairway ascended behind the reception desk located just in front of the elevator. The hotel had everything modern including bedrooms with bath and steam heat! Alas, the depression of the 1930's came on with a vengeance and the place was unable to make enough money to pay expenses. The loan company foreclosed and took possession. The rest of the Lakeway's history was "checkered" by many owners and various styles of operation. It did have a glorious beginning in '29 but soon wilted in the withering '30's.

35- OLD NEIGHBORS, NEIGHBORHOODS AND FRIENDS

The Oliver Norman place is empty. The old concrete part that had the Artesian water flowing through a concrete tank is yet there! I can remember so many good times in that house with all the children of Julia and Howard Norman, Sr. The last ones to live there were Bill and Gertrude. It had a marvelous marsh all along the north side of it where birds and waterfowl nested. Sometimes even some chickens would nest there and raise little chicks. The children called them "wildfowl!" That marsh was a wonderland for my children because plants from "cattails" to trees grew there in such thick abundance, the place was almost a jungle! In fact, "Tarzan" of the comic books was the character they most often imitated in their swinging from tree to tree. Louise Cope and I had many a laugh over our little "apes'" trying to be Tarzan who more often resembled the apes that he was supposed to tame. The good part of such play was that it was outdoors. Noise did not make a problem and there was no limit to the imagination of what an ape could accomplish. We had pretty inventive children! One time they were trekking through the old barn—surrounded by jungle, so it was a part of ape-land, when they decided to climb the ladder into the hayloft. My youngest was about five and bringing up the rear of the line. She fell from the top step of the ladder and landed, bottom first, on the tines of a pitchfork. Late on a Sunday was not a good time to find Dr. Robb. Louise and I put some tincture of iodine on the puncture wound and found we had worked magic. She quit crying as soon as we treated the injury. Ignorance was bliss because she could have developed tetanus or some other infection, but did not. Her only complaint next day was a sore bottom!

Old houses have a way of falling down unless someone has a purpose for them! That eventually happened to the George Fowler house in the town named for him. I had lived there during my twelve years of marriage to Frank Cope. It was an old house then and hopelessly shabby. Gail Norris rented it from me and later bought and remodeled it. After he sold it, someone decided it was not to be "fixed up" again and tore it down, replacing it with a nice mobile home. The brick garage and the roundtop shed on that site are still standing and kept in good repair. That shed was the center of tremendous activity when we lived there! We stored machinery, trucks, supplies—almost everything we owned, including our saddles and horse feed, in that roundtop. Fowler citizens didn't mind goats, chickens or cows and horses in their midst as long as the premises were clean. You could say that was in the days "B.Z."—before zoning! Actually we kept our horse across the road in Dr. Robb's pasture and the cow, too, when we had one. The goats made too much "mischief" and had to go. I don't remember who took them off our hands. It was a great relief to me! They were always "bleating" in a pitiful voice, even immediately after eating. They jumped up on the cloth top of our 1931 Touring car and that sealed their fate. Frank took action to get rid of them that very day. Cars, especially his own, were very important to him—bread and butter in fact. We had no goats in 1933 when he died. I can't remember just when the little creatures left us. I just remember it was "good riddance."

Dorothy and Ralph Dewell lived across the road to the north of the Fowler house and were our dear neighbors. As I recall, her aunt's husband, Dr. Robb, owned the house. It was part of a farmstead on the northwest edge of town. Nine Dewell children were raised there and grew up to be much like their wonderful parents. They lost a three-year-old child in a wash boiler full of hot water—a real tragedy for them. Dorothy and Ralph proved that you could raise your children without all the parental help (as I'd had) and even a big family could turn out well. They taught self- reliance and exercised the old Puritan Ethic. I would not have traded Dorothy for any other neighbor under the sun. She was such a jewel. I learned so much just by observing her. Her efficiency was so matter-of-fact and her "child psychology" was the practical kind! It worked!

The Andor Eliason farm, established in the Artesian Valley in 1879, was a "showplace" by 1910. During his thirty-five years in the county, the man left his mark! The barn was built like a Norwegian fortress must have been—though I never saw one. It had huge timbers supporting the second-story hayloft. They must have been twelve by fourteen inches and held up by verticals of the same proportion. No one in our family had ever seen anything like that barn. Even Uncle Fremont marveled at the construction. The steep roof had a giant Cupola, bigger than a large dog would need as a doghouse. Mr. Eliason spared no expense and no labor! He wanted his cows to be cozy and truly they must have been happy in that barn. He filled the loft in summer and fed out of it in the winter, in true Norwegian fashion.

His house was one-story frame for awhile, white, of course. As he felt more prosperous, he added on another story. The place looked big to me, even bigger than my parents' four-bedroom, two-story, built in 1906.

Eliason's reared eight children in that house. It was inherited by their two daughters, Sena Hankins and Carrie Richardson McGee. They left it to Carrie's daughter, Helene Steele so it's still in the Eliason family.

Near the Eliason farm, farther west, Franklin Marrs and his wife, Amy Rebecca Bryan, settled about 1886. He came in '85 and built a dugout about two miles northeast of Meade. After his wife came in '86, they built a better dugout. All their children were born in their dugouts! Finally the family got a two-room building from the abandoned town of Jaspar, moving it overland on skids. It was their first frame house and above ground. Quite an improvement! In 1911 they built an 11 room mansion, a large two-story, frame house and surrounded it with beautiful trees. Their son, Chester, married Edith Brock, daughter of Jim Brock, an early settler. They brought up their children near to Franklin and Rebecca's beautiful farmstead, along the same road.

Another son, Warren Marrs' descendents still live here. A son, Ralph, married Rosie McGuire. Rosie's sister, Mazo, was buried in the Crooked Creek Cemetery. Ralph and Rosie named their daughter for the baby sister who died. She lives in Gray County, married to Aaron Eccleston. Roy Marrs, Ralph's son stayed in the valley. His son, Duke, lives in Ralph n' Rosie's lovely big house and he has made many improvements to that beautiful old farmstead built by Franklin Marrs.

I can't remember when I did *not* know Lela Marrs, who was Mrs. George Harris. Some of her grandchildren still live in the county. She was such an admirable lady and a true friend. We belonged to the same church in Fowler, our children went to the same school and, after I married Will Merkle, we were members of the same homemakers' club. It is amazing how many "roots" we put down if we stay in the same community all our lives, as I've done! Many of the women I knew as children and later as young matrons, matured with the years and were dependable pillars of the community as we became "senior" citizens. That term "senior" was only recently applied to a class of people over sixty-five who used to be called "old folks." When I was growing up, it never occurred to me that I would someday be one of the "old folks." I can't believe that I have lived so long. I only believe it when I look in a mirror or when I drive through this part of the county and view the farms I once knew. When I drive through Dodge City, Minneola, Fowler, Meade, Plains or Liberal, I realize "how *times have changed*!" and "how *things* have changed!" Some things are better—transportation being one that is. Some things are NOT necessarily better—just different! The little towns have fewer stores to shop in, fewer choices you can make and fewer people to enjoy the friendly, small-town feel. "Gadgets" are better than in the earlier years! I like being able to call from coast-to-coast or to another country but I miss some of the friendliness I knew when we had a Central Switchboard with a friendly person on the line to communicate our needs. Our community used to be tied together by cross-country telephone lines. My dad and Grandad Tullis even hooked up the old magneto telephones to barbed wire that fenced the pastures between our house, his house and Aunt Grace's house. That was before the Bell Company put up the rural phone lines.

36- THE ARRIVAL OF MA BELL

After Bell came out into the country, we subscribed to their "service," a distinct improvement. I still recall our number was "1-3-F-2-4." The 2-4 indicated the number of rings on the party line: two long rings followed by two short rings. It may sound primitive but believe me, it was a great advancement over anything we had prior to that time!

Nellie Martin was our "Central" operator for years. She was called "Central." If anyone had an emergency, he could rely on Nellie to get him help one way or another. She was a faithful, public servant when it came to informing the public of any news of general interest and for the common good. She always gave "general rings" on the party lines to notify people of a fire or other emergency in their neighborhood—or any event. She would put out "general rings" to announce the arrival at the Rock Island Depot of a carload of potatoes, apples, fish or other commodity that could only be brought in quantity by railroad cars. *We didn't have cross-country trucking on any large scale before World War II. We were so dependent upon railroads as the lifelines of the entire country—not just small areas, but the whole country.* Rails brought life to rural America and the small-town telephone central operators brought news of arrival to the town by way of "general rings" on the party lines!

These "general rings" required a lot of extra time and work on Nellie's part but she always did her job willingly, smilingly and beyond the limits of her paid duties. She never spared herself to get the job done! At some point during World War II, Jenny Covey and her daughters, Viola and Marie, took over running the Central Office.

Mrs. Martin's health was failing. They did a wonderful job of carrying on her tradition of exceptional service.

"Bill" Middleswart was tragically widowed in an accident at the new Fowler swimming pool and had a "hard row to hoe" – no job and four small kids to bring up—1936. Her war job in Kansas City ended in 1946. She came back to Fowler as the Central operator at Bell Telephone. Her real name, Anna Juanita, was hardly known because her dad had nicknamed her as a small child. Bill did an admirable job as "Central" operator, assisted by Pauline Beard who had survived *spina bifida* with severe muscle damage. They ran the telephone office efficiently and way above and beyond "the call of duty." They looked upon their jobs as "duty" and did them admirably. I had great respect for "Bill" because I had walked in those leaded boots of "no education" and "little children to support." She reared her four little ones, Joan, Jean, Joyce and J. C. to adults in their home community. She married Harvey Way in 1961, after rearing her family. In my eyes, she was a woman who responded nobly to the challenge put upon her by circumstances.

Nelle Bradley was the last Central Operator. She had been the chief operator at Meade for many years before she came to run the Fowler office. She stayed with the job until she had a bad fall, breaking both wrists. Then son Richard and his wife, Norma, filled in. You could say that they were the last ones to run the switchboard. Never was a small town more blest with high performing, ethical and honorable telephone operators than Fowler! Probably there were others that were but I just never heard about them.

37- CRIME ON THE PRAIRIE

When you have lived so long, there are so many memories of friends, places and things that happened. The good and the bad seem to leave a mark for remembrance. They were not all good.

Rosetta Bunyan Way, was an example of courage and endurance. Rosetta was what I would call a "graduate" from the *school of hard knocks.* She was eleven years older than I and had lost her mother in 1894. Talk about a tragedy—that was one! The three little girls were all at home; Viola was about thirteen, Rosetta, six and Maud, four. Their dad, William P. Bunyan, had gone to Dodge City from their place just north of Fowler on Crooked Creek, when a lone horseman evidently spied the rancher leaving and rode into the homestead site. He quickly overpowered Bunyan's wife, Laura, threatening to kill her if she resisted. The man put the three girls outside without shoes so they could not go for help. He then proceeded to rape the young woman, biting her viciously on her upper body. Somehow, the terrified woman managed to get to her husband's loaded Winchester. She knew how to fire it and did so, at close range, ending the attack abruptly and forever.

The little girls were terrified at the sight of their mother's wounds but managed to help her drag the body outside their sod house. On his return next day, her horrified husband found poor Laura in a terrible condition and tried to find someone to help. Unfortunately, her wounds soon produced fever, swelling and pain. In spite of medical care, poor at that time, she died of infection about two months later, on December 30, 1894. It was called "blood poisoning" in those days.

Today it's "septicemia." But now there are antibiotics to stop it. At that time, there was nothing that worked. People tried cauterizing and all kinds of "poultices" to no avail. Three little girls were without a mother and their father felt helpless, enraged, desperate and grieved. He showed all his emotions and tried to make the best of a terrible situation, over-indulging his daughters while hoping to find a mother for them. The girls became very spoiled and selfish—with dad's help.

He married a niece of George Fowler soon after Laura's death but her family had the marriage annulled for reasons not apparent to outsiders. Six years later he married another young woman, Lea Finley. She produced a son, William Price Bunyan, Jr. Lea's three step-daughters were out of hand and would never accept her as a mother figure. They had learned to manage their father in their own way and wanted no other woman in the home. As a result, all the daughters married older men when they were quite young, "to get away from home."

At fourteen, Rosetta married Marion M. Way, twelve years her senior. She had her first child, Laura, at age fifteen, in 1903. Harvey was born in 1905 and Irma in 1906. Both little daughters died, Laura at age three and Irma, at one year. Her son, Harvey, was precious to her but was not enough to hold the marriage together.

Although divorce was not socially acceptable at that time, Rosetta decided to leave an untenable situation. She demonstrated her grit by taking up nursing as a profession, earning her title as a Registered Nurse. That was very hard work for a woman in her thirties; but she had already been through a great deal of suffering and seemed to have her father's ability to endure whatever came along. After her son no longer needed her, Rosetta moved to California, where she worked as a Public Health Nurse. She drove back to Kansas several times to visit her son with her sister's two sons, Ralph and Fred Hamer, coming along. She was a good story-teller and told of her work in California in a very entertaining way. She worked in a part of Los Angeles County where migrant laborers made up most of the population. Share-croppers from the deep South had settled in great numbers in low priced housing units. Plumbing was a mystery to them, as was any other modern convenience.

Once she told of a routine visit with a family from Arkansas, where she detected a terrible smell coming from a bedroom closet. She found a hole cut in the floor. The family had converted the closet to a latrine. They were using the flush toilet as a "foot-bath" and thought it was a wonderful way to soak their feet when they came in from the fields. She said she learned never to be surprised at anything on those public health visits. The migrant sharecroppers had not had an opportunity to learn. Life had always been a work-if-you-want-to-eat situation. Coming from the rural South to California was an experience to get used to and it didn't happen overnight. Some people made fortunes off the stories they told about the migration to California.

I remember reading John Steinbeck's novel Grapes of Wrath. It must have been a pretty faithful portrayal of how life was in the migrant communities. That was pretty similar to the way my friend, Rosetta told it. If she had written all the things she told me, she could have had a best-selling novel!

Absalom Hadlock homesteaded his place two miles north of the creek about 1896. His children were Lilllie, Sarah, Lucinda, Robert and Moses, the youngest. Lillie married Oliver Latta and Sarah married his brother Virgil. Effie Latta, sister to Oliver and Virge, married Dell Wetmore who came in 1891. Lucinda married a Hockett. Robert moved to Washington state before he was married, I think. The Hadlock farm is still occupied by Moses' daughter, Ila Hadlock, who married Charles "Chuck" Edwards, a descendent of George Edwards and his wife, McOlin M. Mathis, who settled in the Artesian Valley in the spring of 1885. Chuck and Ila's son, Steve Edwards, lives three miles south on what was once A.C. and Olive Tillman's farm, which Olive inherited from her father, Clarence Harner. It is located eleven miles north and two east of Meade.

A mile or two below Hadlock's, almost on the banks of Crooked Creek, was the place homesteaded by John Conrad and his wife, Freelove McAlister, in 1879. He was a cattleman and believed in open range. Eventually the Conrad's found themselves surrounded by farmers who fenced their cropland. There were a lot of "misunderstandings" among Conrad and his neighbors—my parents included, but somehow, after it was all said and done, they became very close-knit friends and neighbors.

My mother, Jessie Tullis McCauley, was very fond of "Sweetie" Conrad, whose real name was also Jessie. They were good friends all their lives. "Sweetie" married Jim Maynard, who hailed from Iowa where his family had known the Tullises. She and Jim moved to Iowa after their marriage but returned to Fowler in 1936. Jim farmed the Conrad land along Crooked Creek for many years. His daughter, Mona Ratzlaff, lived in a house very near the creek, that was actually the old McCauley school house, moved from Section 1-30-27, that had belonged to Uncle Fremont.She and her husband, Henry "Hank" Ratzlaff, built a couple of rooms onto that school house and reared their children there after WWII.

No one lives there anymore. No one lives on the Conrad place. There are so many farms where empty buildings stand like monuments to a past that doesn't exist anymore! My heart aches to see so many deserted places. In my memory, they're all so vivid and full of life!

Farther east on the creek stands the Chipman place, deserted. Then the Salmon place, where Henry and Lucy Salmon had lived for years. Then their son, Ira, and his wife, Agnes Golliher, lived many years and reared their children there. Agnes was such a darling person. Everyone loved her. She was the daughter of Jerry Golliher, an early-day native son. I think the Golliher family came to Kansas around 1888 but actually settled in Meade County around 1910.

Farther down the creek was the Beckerman farm, about a mile south of where my uncle, Walter Tullis, lived. Beckerman's joined my parents' pasture on the west side. They lived almost in the bottom of Crooked Creek. They were devout Catholics and raised a large family. I remember Ben, Fred, John, and the two younger girls, Regina and Johanna. I know there was an older girl or two who became nuns but can't remember their names. Just two miles north on that same road, another Catholic family lived. I remember some of their children well—Pete and Louie, Mildred and Marie Fox. My dad was very fond of Pete and Louie Fox. I always thought it was interesting that, for someone reared by Congregationalists who were such avid anti-Catholics, he seemed to be completely untainted by their prejudice, getting along extremely well with all his Catholic neighbors and they seemed to like him in return. They exchanged work at times, as neighbors often did. They were always congenial.

The Lepels lived a mile east of us for several years. Posie and I were "best friends." She was the youngest of her dad's first family. He married again and they moved over northeast of Fowler. In World War I, that place was owned by Henry and Binnie Cope, who became my in-laws. It was later bought by Bill Reese. I don't know who owns it now but there's no house or anything resembling a farmstead there now.

The Andrew J. McCauley farm with its two big houses, side by side, was leveled by the man who bought it after WWII. All those trees, barns and outbuildings were just dozed down where my cousin Andrew and Uncle Forest had put in so much toil. Not one tree of that timber claim was left standing! That still gives me a twinge to drive by it. I had so many wonderful memories of Aunt Flo and of Andrew's wife Edna. We were close. It hurt me terribly to see them leave in 1939.

Uncle Fremont's house, built in 1907, still stands just south of the creek and has been remodeled and improved, still occupied by the Lees' descendents. It was a three-story giant without any trees around it. Fremont liked his trees in timber claims! He was not a person to dwell on aesthetics. Practicality and efficiency were important to him.

Farther east, Carl Haywood's place was back north of the creek more than a mile. He and Edith had a fine, big house on it in the 1920's.It had the big porch, typical of the '20's. Carl and my dad were always good friends and neighbors. Their daughter, Nettie, and I were always best of friends. I missed her when she moved to California in the '30's. She married Paul Younger, a preacher, so moved several times after her marriage!

Clarence and Elsie Haywood had a beautiful, two-story, gabled house on their place, surrounded by fruit trees. It was two or three miles farther east and was quite beautiful. They reared their two boys, Harold and Bob; later Harold and his wife, Loretta Dabbelt, reared theirs in the same house. Bob became a history professor and spent most of his adult life in Topeka. He wrote several historical books while he was at Washburn University and after he retired.

Other large, two story houses that used to be pretty were the Long's, M.M.Ways' and the J.E. Little's. Chester Long had been a U.S. Senator and put a lot of money into his farm in the 1920's. He had great dreams for his farm but his sons didn't take to farming the way he had hoped. His grandson Lyman's wife, Nancy, took her own life there during WWII. It was one of those sad tales you wish you didn't remember.

Almost all families, if you know them for more than one generation, will have some sad stories to relate. The folks along Crooked Creek were no different. They saw their share of sadness. Aunt Belle and Uncle Howard Gilchrist ended their lives almost as paupers. She didn't even have a tombstone to mark her final resting place because 1936 was the peak of the hard times! Probably no one earns less than an itinerant preacher did in those days. Howard Gilchrist had spent his entire life preaching and much of that time he was a circuit rider.

His last "contract" with a church was in Meade, at the First Baptist Church, shortly before he died. If he had lived, that would have been his last pastorate. Alas, it didn't turn out that way. He died before he could fulfill his contract. Aunt Belle, bless her soul, preached many a sermon to anyone who would listen but she was never ordained. Preaching just came naturally to her. I can see her still—standing at the window, believing that the Lord might come back that very night.

If it hadn't been for her prosperous brother, Uncle Charlie, Belle and Howard might have gone hungry a few times. However, he took care of them and considered it his privilege and his sacred duty.

When my youngest was six, Aunt Belle heard her play the organ she kept in the parlor. She immediately wanted Ellen to have that organ. We had no place to put it and I had to say "No" to the gift. That was a "sore spot" with my daughter for many years. She never let me forget that she would have loved to have that instrument. It had been kept in perfect condition and would have been worth a great deal as an "antique" now but even more as a family keepsake.

By age sixteen, she was playing the organ at the Episcopal Church in Meade for regular Sunday services. The instrument she played had belonged to Nellie Sourbier Brannan and was not in nearly as good condition as the one Aunt Belle had offered her! My hindsight was better than my foresight. I don't even recall what happened to the instrument Aunt Belle had! I do recall some of the hymns I heard played on it, however, and they're as fresh in my mind as the day I heard them. I learned to play some of the simpler ones but I was never much of an organist! The words seem to be indelible though.

"O saving Victim, opening wide   The Gate of heav'n to man below, Our foes press on from every side, Thine aid supply, thy strength bestow..

"All praise and thanks to Thee ascend, Forevermore, blest one in three; O grant us life that shall not end, In our true native land with thee!" (Thomas Aquinas,1263)

Looking back, I realize how right my great-Aunt Belle was about so many things. What a wonderful world we would have if we could all have had her faith and perseverance!

* *

Appendix I-Family Trees of Early Settlers along Crooked Creek and in the Artesian Valley

<u>B</u>

<u>Bunyan, William Price</u> 1862 -1934 (arrived in KS, 1879)

<u>Married: (first) Laura,</u> 1863-1894. Issue: three daughters

<u>Viola</u> b. 1881; m. Fred Hamar,Sr.

<u>Maud</u> 1886-1979; m. van Riper; m.___Elliott.

<u>Rosetta</u> 1888-1958; m. Marion M. Way,1876 -1949.

      Issue:Laura,1903-1906; Harvey 1905-1972; Irma, 1906-1907.

<u>Married: (second) m. Anna_____</u>(niece of George Fowler,)1899,

      Marriage anulled by her family.

<u>Married: (third) m.</u> Lea Finley, 1899.

      Issue one son:<u>William P. Bunyan, Jr(1910-1967)m.Loraine Gregory</u>

      Sons: William P.III; Gregory Bunyan

      Issue of Greg: Lori Finke, Sara Hayes, Mikealea

<u>C</u>

<u>Conrad, John Francis(1848-1936) m.Freelove McAllister, (1854-1921)</u>

<u>Issue</u>:Lucy, 1878, Joseph E. (1880-1924) Whitney (1884-1939)Jessie (1886-1970).

      <u>Lucy Conrad m. Henry Lyon Salmon (1864-1947) 1898,</u>

<u>Issue</u>:Mary E. Dalgarn; Anna B. Veeder; Ira F. Salmon; Leonard L. Salmon; Eleanor Jones; Alice Hoffman, Betty Jo Endicott.

      <u>Jessie Conrad m. James L. "Jim" Maynard (Iowa) 1912.</u>

<u>Issue</u>: Enid Willis, James L., Mona Ratzlaff , John W.

C

Cope , Francis Bryan(Frank)(1893-1933)m. Helen L. McCauley, 1921.

Issue:Wanda C.Cope b.1922;WayneMcCauleyCope1925-1998;Luellen L.Cope, b.1929

Wanda C. Cope m. Walter L. Lewis, 1943;Issue: Richard W. b, 1945; Ronald W. b.1948; Shelley L. b. 1950; Kyle S. b.1956.

Wayne M.Cope (first)m. 1950-Pauline Hunt, Issue: Paula C. b. 1951; (second) m. 1960- Sammy King; (adopted daughter of Sammy) Stacy..

Luellen L. b.1929; (1st) m 1949-J. D. Boyd,1931-1974 Issue:Bradley 1953,Barbara 1957. $2^{nd\,m.}$ Richard Verell 1982. No issue.

HenryCopeJr(Harry)1896-1956 m.LouiseM.Norman, 1922

Issue:George b.1923; Norma b.1925, Dorothy b.1927

George m. Madalyn-----;Issue: Tanya, Wendy

Norma m. Russell Wiitala; Issue: Sonja, Teresa, Russell, Jr.

Dorothy m. Durand Cole; Issue: Georgette; Julie

E

Eliason, Andor b.1844 -1914; m. Helena M.(1850-1947)

Children in birth order: Lena Innis 1871-1921; Julia Norman ; Amelia m.Ericson; John, 1880-1929 [first white child born in Meade County;] Emaus "Pete", 1882-1925; m. Emma Coon; Caroline "Carrie"(Richardson) McGee,1884-1980; Mary m. John Wood; Eva ,m.Tom Gray; Anna E. "Sena" 1890-1977, m. Dr. Hankins;

H

Haywood, Benjamin Franklin, (1844-1918) No issue.

Haywood, Charles E. Sr.(1856-1923)m.MarthaHutchinson (1863-1935)

Issue: Carl, Clarence, Nettie Younger

Issue of Carl and Edith Scott:Louis,Bernita McKissick, Charles,

Issue of Clarence and Elsie Long Haywood: Harold B., C.Robert.

Issue of Nettie and Paul Younger_____

L

Lepel, Frank Herman m. Elizabeth Mary Ohlman (d.1904)

Moved to Meade County from Caldwell, Kansas, after migrating to Canada and returning. After death of Elizabeth Mary, buried in the Crooked Creek Cemetery, he married again to _____ who raised his children and had _____more.

Children of Frank and Elizabeth Mary: Frank Leopold; Farnia, Charlie, Mary Elizabeth, Ohlman, Paul, Posie Violet

M

Marrs, Franklin m. Amy Rebecca Bryan

Issue: Ott, Warren, Ralph, Chester, Lela, Fannie, Edna

Ott Marrs m. Maude Pittman

Warren Marrs m. Feryl Flynn m.(second) Mabel Fuhrman

Issue 1st: Aileen, Guinola Tacha, Alfred, Leola Brown, Warrenetta Fisher, Lavon Miller, Betty Leis, Virgil, Wendell

Ralph Marrs m. Rosie McGuire

Issue: Roy, Marion, Franklin, Ruby Whatley, Rosetta Thompson, Ida Eikerman, Mazo Eccleston

Chester Marrs m. Edith Brock

Issue; Lloyd, Irvin, Pauline, Roscoe (d.WWII,) Richard, Ella Mae, Louis,

Lela Marrs m. George Harris

Issue:LaVeta McManamon, William "Bill"

Fannie Marrs, m. W.J. "Pete" Hardaway

Issue:Florence,Velma,Ruth,Juanita,Yvonne, Loren, Maudessa, Dean, Warren,

Edna Marrs, m. _____Flint

M

Merkle, William John (1897-1983)m.Helen McCauley Cope, 6/24/42

Children: Wm. J. adopted Ellen Cope in 1945.

Parents: William Merkle (born Wilhelm Merkel in Germany) and Catherine Wolfley

Other children of William and Catherine Wolfley Merkle:

Matilda Merkle m.Orville Johnson; Issue:George,Orval,Mary,Alice,Iola,Lola,

Grace m. Howard E. Weller; Issue: Bernard E.

George m. Edna McBee; Issue: Owen, Farran D.

Charles m. Hazel Kintner; Issue: Beverly Rogers

Carl m. Phronie Spendin; Issue: Sharon Stockton

Augustus m. Rita Meng; Issue: Mary Ann Burns

Mc

McCauley, Andrew Jackson, Sr.(1833-1885)

Married: 1854 to Mary Brown (b. England)

Issue: Helen,1855-1897 m. Hervey Forbes

       Issue: Will McCauley; Maude, Walter Forbes

John C.Fremont(1857-1937)m. Mary Bateman No issue

Arabella (Belle)(1859-1936)m. Howard Gilchrist; Issue:Harold,Mary,Nellie

Wesley B. b.1861 moved to Florida/no return

Andrew Jr. (1863-1885)(never married)

Charles D. McCauley (1865-1933)(never married)

Forrest (1867-1952) m. Florence Davis Issue:Warren,Andrew,Stella,Albert,Mildred

Nellie Grace (1870-71)

N

Norman, Oliver, m. Araminta ,(d. 1905,) came to Meade County in 1879, settling in the Artesian Valley

Issue:Howard, Will, John, Eliza "Dolly", Ellen

Howard Norman, Sr. (d. 1936) m. Julia Eliason (d.1958)

Dolly (Eliza J.) m.John Jobling; Issue: Wm."Bill" Jobling, d.1944.

Ellen m.Hume McGinnis;

John and Will moved back to Sumner County in 1905.

Issue of Howard and Julia (Eliason) Norman:

Louise 1st m. Henry J.(Harry) Cope; 2nd m. Loren Beach

Mary m.Ted Olsten, (moved - California.) Howard Jr., m. Geraldine Coon

Gladys m. Sheldon Newkirk (California, then Oregon)

William m 1st .Evelyn Pullman; m.2nd Gertrude Lepel

Jamie m.Vaughn Kachadorian (moved - California)

Issue of Howard Jr. and Geraldine (Coon) Norman:

David b.1938, m.Irene Newkirk

Christine (1940-85) m. Kenneth Weber

Pat b.1942, m. OdusTrober; m.LarryZwickle

Michael b.1945 m. Sandy Dodd

Issue of William and Gertrude (Lepel) Norman:

Gary b. 1951, m.Marilyn Calub,m.Sally_____ (moved-Oregon)

Russell b. 1954, m.Carla Easley Miller (moved-Arkansas)

William Norman, b. 1955, m.Donna Balls

Trudy, b.1961, m. Michael Kemper

T-Tullis

Charles W. (1856-1936), m. Eva McCabe, (1858-1928)1878, Iowa

Children: Jessie Luella, (1879-1958) m. Will E. McCauley 1898, Gray County,Kansas, Issue: Helen L. McCauley

Wiley J. b.1881,m. Alma Gresham, Issue: Velma, Charles, Carl

Edna_b. 1883 m. Frank Wilhite, Issue: Harold, Finis, Franklin,Wanda, Freda

Grace b.1888, m. Paskel Spivey, Issue: Loyde

Walter E. b.1891, m. Pearl Gamble, Issue: Onis (Eccleston)

W-WATERS

Bohler Cullison Waters, m. Sarah Bohr, (b.Pennsylvania to John Devon Bohr of Amish faith.)

Issue: Grace, Mae, Devon, Bill, Helen

Grace m. Howard Sumner

Issue: Lucille, Ernest, Howard Jr., Harvey,

May m. Theron Rexford

Issue: Alva, Chester, Lois

Samuel Devon m._____; Issue: Dick, Ted

Ted m. Dana Poteet; Issue: Jeff, Shane

William "Bill" Britton Waters m. Vera Harper (no issue)

Helen m. Walter John Dierking; m. Homer Jenkinson

Issue: Georgia Lee Dierking

W

Wetmore, Dell, settled here ,1891, from Wisconson ;m. Effie Latta_,came 1884;

<u>Issue: Joseph</u> m. Adeline Unruh; (no issue)

<u>Charlotte</u> m. Harold Wilcox; Issue: Vernadell, Georgiabell, Janice, John, Roe,

Clifford Wetmore m. Florence Wright;Issue: Ruth, Frank, Fay

<u>Ruth m.</u>Ira Doyle, issue: Cheryl; later m. _____Smith; <u>Fay,</u> no issue; d.age 19.

<u>Frank m.</u> Marlene Brown Issue: Sandra, David, Jan

Appendix II

Certificate of Ordination Issued by First Baptist Church of Meade to the Rev. Howard H.Gilchrist

"Pursuant to the call of the First Baptist Church of Meade, Kansas, a Council met at 3:30 p.m. of February 18th, 1906, to consider the advisability of setting apart Brother Howard H. Gilchrist, a member of the Church to the work of the gospel ministry among Baptist Churches.

"The Council consisted of the representation of the Meade Baptist Church and Rev. E.B. Meredith, the General Missionary for Kansas, no other churches having responded with delegates.

"The Council organized by electing E.B. Meredith, Moderator and Bro. C.S. Hulburt, Clerk.

After listening to a statement by Rev. Gilchrist of his Christian experience, call to the ministry and views of Christian doctrines, it was unanimously voted that we express ourselves as satisfied with these statements and that we proceed by public services, prayer and the laying on of hands to set Brother Howard H. Gilchrist apart to the work of the Gospel ministry.

Done at Meade, Kansas   (signed)   E.B.Meredith,   Moderator

February 18th, 1906   C.S.Hulburt   Clerk

J. M. Robinson, Pastor, First Baptist Church; Meade, Kansas

Baptist Church, Meade,Kansas

Glossary of Information

C

Crash of 1929. Occurred 24 October, 1929. The stock market on Wall Street in New York suffered irreparable losses in which thousands of companies were destroyed and millions of Americans lost all they had invested in the companies. A similar crash occurred in 1896 but on a much smaller scale.

F

Fair Labor Standards Act, passed by Congress, 24 October, 1938, created a 40 hour work week and established a minimum wage of 25 cents/hour.

N

Newspapers, Fowler

June 1885-91	The Fowler Graphic	E. E. Henley
	The Fowler Advocate	
1906-1914	The Fowler Gazette	I. J. Stanton
1914-	The Fowler Gazette	W. R. Bond
Sold	The Fowler News	Perry Brothers
1931	The Fowler News	Ted J. Gardner
1972	The Fowler News	Jerry Anderson

Newspapers, Meade

4/15/1879	The Pearlette Call	Bennett & Lowery
May, 1885	The Spring Lake Hornet	C. K. Sourbier
July, 1885	The Meade Center Press	Cannon Brothers
1885	The Carthage Times	Melcher Brothers
December 1885	The Press Democrat	Melcher Brothers
July, 1885	The Meade County Globe	J. M. Johnson
August, 1886	The Meade County Globe `	W. S. Martin
1887	The Meade Republican	T. J. Palmer
1887	The Mertilla Times	H. L. Bishop
1887	The Meade Center Telegram	Lon Whorton
1890	The Meade Democrat	Sam Lawrence
1894	The Meade Democrat	C. G. Allen

1/11/1900 Meade County News	E.D.Smith,John Miller,Agnes Wehrle
November,1913 The Meade County Globe	John Wehrle
1912-1918 The Meade County News	Agnes and GeoWehrle
1918 Meade County Globe consolidated with Meade County News	
1918-1926 The Meade Globe News	Agnes and Geo. Wehrle
1926 The Meade Globe News	Keith Cox
October, 1931 The Meade County Press	George and Pearl Carey
1937 The Meade Globe News	Keith Cox & Bill Owens
1954 The Meade Globe News consolidated with Meade County Press	
1954-63 The Meade Globe Press	George and Pearl Carey
1963-72 Meade Globe Press	George and Pearl Carey
1972 Meade Globe Press	Jerry Anderson, publisher
1972-76 Meade Globe Press	John Husband, editor
1976 Meade Globe Press	Kay Milford, editor
1986 Meade County News	Tom Kuhns, editor

"prove up"- building a dwelling. *The Homestead Act of 1862* required that anyone filing a "claim" on 160 acres of land should improve it with a house and live 5 years on the land. To build improvements was to "prove up."

Puritan Ethic- a Doctrine taught in New England by the first Colonists, affirming that if a man feared God, worked hard, was moderate in all things and didn't spend the principal, he would overcome the hazards of a perverse-growing season, beget children and die in old age surround by those same Christian offspring, a full granary and the certain knowledge of eternal salvation. It was a Code of Conduct that prevailed in much of the settlement of the West—Kansas in particular—as it had earlier in the northeastern colonies.

Road Ranch- A wayside station for travelers on a trail. Supplies, meals and sometimes even overnight lodging were made available. Some freighters kept fresh horses at road ranches when making long hauls. Animal feed was kept also.

County Superintendents of Education: (Elective Office)

1886 N. B. Clark, appointed for short term
1886 N. H. Mendenhall
1890 Mollie Dalgarn
1892 D. P. Wysong
1894 Jennie Kessler
1898 J. A Porterfield
1900 Maggie Martin
1904 Ruth Bennett
1908 Mattie Haig
1912 Pearl Wood Smith
1916 Ola Granger
1922 Clara Carrell
1928 Louise Hallock
1932 Mattie Boyd
1936-63 Ola Granger

T

Trails crossing Meade County- leaving the *Santa Fe Trail* near Dodge City, the *Jones and Plummer Trail* ran southwest to a road ranch one mile east of Meade. This road ranch was owned by Hoodo Brown and sold supplies to travelers. Hoodo's youngest daughter, Grace, died and was buried near the road ranch home. In 1885, when he left the area, Brown gave the land to the *Graceland Cemetery Association* in honor or his daughter, Grace. It is *located one mile east of Meade on Highway 54 and still bears the name, Graceland. The Jones and Plummer Trail* goes from Meade southwest to the Odee Post office on the south bank of the Cimarron River, 1 7/8 miles east of State Highway 23, then south to Beaver City, Oklahoma.

The Fort Bascom Trail branched off the Jones and Plummer Trail at Meade in a southwesterly direction.

W-

Water works- public utility providing the water supply to a whole community . This includes wells, storage for water, underground mains, pressurizing flow.

Meade Water Works, example of how public utilities evolve in a new settlement.

In 1885 a Mr. McDonald drilled 4 wells and installed hand pumps for bringing up water. In August, 1899, several citizens went to Springfield, near Liberal, to buy a wooden tower and 4 miles of connecting water mains. The tower was erected at the corner of Carthage and Meade Center. Mains were laid. Tragically, F.M. Rosenberry fell from the top of the tower, some 40 feet, living only about 2 hours.. By July 10,1902, forty people pledged $800 toward development of a water works. Work resumed June, 1903, with a 12 foot Samson windmill erected at the city well. Water was pumped into a big galvanized tank where horses could drink. The public was urged to use great care not to damage the tanks with wagons or buggy tongues. Fire plugs were installed after the mains were laid. All pipes were connected to the 1600 gallon tank. In November, 1903, water was piped to the National Hotel (where the Lakeway Hotel now sits.) A freeze in late November caused many pipes to spring leaks. With so much water use, cesspools began filling up. This raised the question of the need for a proper sewer system. Thus progress demanded more and better improvements, not only of the water system but also to handle the waste.

By 1909, the city's "perfect" water system was in bad condition. The city council discussed the purchase of a steel water tank and tower. In 1911, the old tank was torn down and a steel tower erected on West Carthage. It was replaced by another well and tank in northeast Meade in the mid-1980's.

The advent of propane gas in rural Meade County.

John P. Ballard, a 1903 settler on a claim south of Plains, brought butane gas, the forerunner of propane, to rural Meade County in the late thirties when he decided to move to Plains and go into the butane business. Prior to this, only kerosene lamplight and wood or coal heating was used. What a transformation! My dad installed a gas floor furnace where the coal burning stove had sat. He learned about butane lighting and gas refrigerators from J.P. Ballard and decided those would be a wonderful boon to life in the country. That was 1938, as I recall. What a difference in the life of a housewife to be able to refrigerate foods and to be freed from the task of maintaining the oil-burning light with that delicate mantel and chimney! Rural Electrification (REA) came in about ten years after that, with REA telephones following in 1954.

Appendix III

C.D.McCauley Dies

**Funeral for Beloved Citizen Was Held
at Friends Church Sunday Afternoon.**

C.D. McCauley died Thursday after suffering paralysis two years. One of the most prosperous farmers in this locality, he was a man of great integrity and business acumen and was a director of the Fowler Equity Exchange for many years. He was serving in this capacity at the time of his death.

The community feels the shock of loss of this well known man.

Charles Dwin McCauley was born in Defiance County Ohio, May 10, 1865, and departed this life January 12,1933, at the age of 67 years, 8 mo. and 2 da.

At age nine he moved to Illinois with his family to a farm near Broadwell, in Logan County. In March, 1879, the family came to Kansas, settling in the Crooked Creek valley and being among the earliest settlers.

In 1881-82 he was converted and joined the Crooked Creek Congregational Church and later was the Sunday School Superintendent.

Still later he spent five years in The State College at Manhattan, graduating in 1896.

Since 1901 he has resided on his farm north of Fowler. He never married.

His last illness covered a period of nearly two years, the third stroke coming last Monday eve. All possible loving care was given by his niece, Mrs. Will Ellson, together with her husband and others.

His parents, two brothers and two sisters preceded him in death. Left to mourn his Passing are a sister, Mrs. H.H. Gilchrist, and two brothers, J.C.F. and F.H. McCauley, together with eleven nephews and nieces.

The body will be laid to rest in the McCauley cemetery, there to await the resurrection morn.

The Fowler News, 1/15/1933

Catherine Merkle Obituary

Catherine Rebecca Wolfley was born near Soldier, in Nemaha County, Kansas, January 22, 1867, to Augustus J. and Matilda Wolfley, the fourth child of thirteen.

Moving to Meade county with her parents, she was married to William Merkle, January 2, 1894. To this union were born seven children, Mrs. Matilda Johnson, West Cliff, Colorado and Mrs. Grace Weller, Montezuma, Kans., William, Charles, Carl, George and August, all of the Fowler area.

Mrs. Merkle was a faithful wife and devoted mother. She with her husband battled the trials of life for nearly forty-five years together, enduring pioneer days, yet enjoying the simple beauty and quietude of the plains, doing the things their hands found to do in developing the Western plains.

She was always optimistic and cheerful and made a comfortable home for her family. As the gates of death opened, she paused a moment on the threshold to leave this fare-well message to loved ones. "We don't know why these things happen but God knows best."

She leaves to share this love and memory her beloved husband, children, nine grand-children, five sisters, Mrs. Mattie Convville, West Pt., Oregon; Mrs. Carrie Lewis, Hutchinson; Mrs. Minnie Lewis, Castleton; Mrs. Frances Olson, Hutchinson , Mrs. Mina Padgett, Fowler; and one brother, Jacob Wolfley, Onaga preceded her in death.

Funeral Service in Fowler Christian Church. Interment in Fowler Cemetery Saturday, November 20. Mrs. Mason Glaze officiated.

The Fowler News 11/25/37

Another Pioneer is Called to Eternal Home

Wm. Merkle Passed Away Feb. 1st

In Wurttenberg, Germany, born to the George Merkle family, November 23,1861, A son was given the name William. Just prior to age 14, he came to America with an uncle, taking residence in Virginia. Later he went to Peoria, Illinois, where he lived some years and took steps to become a citizen.

The fall of 1884, at age 23, he came to Meade county from Peabody, Kansas, where he had lived a short time.

In March, 1886, Mr. Merkle Received his final naturalization certificate.

Possessed with a dynamic personality, indomitable will power and boundless energy, He soon became an integral part of his community. His personality was such that it overshadowed all other things around him. He was a man of few words but they always had meaning and he always kept them. He was endowed with kindness, generosity, tolerance, friendliness and with diligence and fortitude beyond what most people are privileged to have.

These qualities enabled him to come to a strange land and carve a small empire.

His education was limited and it was necessary for him to learn the English language, and to read and write it. He attended school a few months in America. By doing much reading and thinking he became exceedingly well-informed.

January 9, 1894, he married Catherine Wolfley, of Fowler. She was brought home to the 3-room sod "mansion" and immediately fell in step with her husband. They never did anything for show. Dependability was written on their faces and associated with their presence.

Survivors are two daughters, Matilda Johnson and Grace Weller, five sons, William J., George, Charles, Carl and August, ten grandchildren and five great-grandchildren. Funeral services were at Fowler Christian Church, Feb.4, with Rev. Mrs. Mason Glaze assisted by Rev. Behler.
(Fowler News)2/8/40

William J. Merkle

William J. Merkle, 86, of Meade, died Aug.16, 1983, at Meade Hospital. He was born April 11, 1897, in Meade County and was a lifelong county resident.

Mr. Merkle was a World War I veteran. He married Helen L. McCauley June 24, 1941 at Garden City. He was a farmer and stockman.

Survivors include the widow, a daughter, Ellen Verell of Tulsa, Oklahoma; step-daughter, Wanda Lewis, Fowler; step-son Wayne Cope, Liberal; sister Grace Weller and two brothers, Carl and George, all of Meade; eight grandchildren and 11 great grandchildren.

Funeral services will be at 9:30 a.m. Thursday at Fidler-Orme Mortuary, Meade, with the Rev. Gayland Aubrey officiating. Burial will be in Fowler cemetery. Suggested memorial contributions to St. Francis Boys Home, Salina, in care of Fowler State Bank. *(Meade Globe-Press)*

Helen L. Merkle

Helen L. Merkle, 96, died Oct 6, 1996, at Bethel Home, Montezuma.

She was born Oct.15, 1899, in a sod house on her parents' claim in Gray County, the daughter of Will E. and Jessie Tullis McCauley. A lifetime Meade County resident, she was a farmer and homemaker and member of St. Augustine Episcopal Church, Meade.

On Sept.21,1921, she married Francis B. Cope at Cimarron. He died in 1933. On June 24, 1941, she married William J. Merkle at Garden City. He died Aug.16, 1983.

Survivors: son, Wayne Cope, Liberal; daughters Wanda Lewis, Fowler, and Ellen Verell, Meade. Eight grandchildren; 12 great-grandchildren and a great-great granddaughter. Funeral will be 2 p.m. Wednesday at Fowler Cemetery with the Rev. James Johnson presiding. Memorials may be sent to Bethel Home, Montezuma or to St. Francis Boys Home, Salina. *(Meade County News, 10/8/96)*

Early Settler, Mrs. Jessie McCauley

Passed Away March 24 at Meade.

Mrs. W.E. McCauley of Meade died at Meade Hospital March 24, 1958, at age 79. She was born in Lee County, Iowa, Feb.21, 1879.

Mrs. McCauley had come with her parents to Hamilton County in 1887, then to Gray County in 1894. She married Will McCauley in 1898 at her parents' home on Crooked Creek on the Meade-Gray County line.

Survivors are: her husband, Will, a daughter, Helen Merkle, two grand-daughters, Wanda Lewis and Ellen Boyd and grandson, Wayne Cope, Liberal, and seven grandchildren. Also: a brother, Walter Tullis, Fowler, sisters, Grace Spivey, Hutchinson, and Edna Wilhite, Long Beach, Calif.
Her parents, Charles and Eva Tullis, Fowler, and one brother, Wiley Tullis, Fowler, preceded her.
Services were conducted Mar.26 by Capt. Oliver Parkes at the Meade Christian Church, with burial in Graceland Cemetery, Meade.
(*Meade Globe-News*, 3/28/58)

W.E. McCauley, Died Dec.26 at Meade District Hospital.

Will E. McCauley, 86, died at Meade Hospital after a brief illness, Dec.26, 1962. He was an early settler, having come to the Crooked Creek Community north of Fowler at age 4 with his mother and grandparents in 1879.

He grew up at Arkalon on the Cimarron River, working as a cowboy from his early teens.

 He married Jessie L. Tullis of Gray County, in February,1898. The two built their sod home during their first year, living in an abandoned dugout on the Jones and Plummer trail on Crooked Creek. His wife died in 1958. They had lived in Meade since 1947.

Survivors are his daughter and son-in-law, Helen and William Merkle, granddaughters, Wanda Lewis and Ellen Boyd, grand-son Wayne Cope, Liberal, and eight grandchildren.

Burial was in Graceland Cemetery.
(*Meade Globe-Press,* 12/29/63)

Appendix IV

Clippings from other sources...

McCAULEY

by Helen Merkle, daughter of the late W.E. McCauley

In 1879, the McCauley family, Andrew Sr. and wife Mary, together with their five sons, two daughters and four-year-old grandson, Willie, joined a wagon train in Illinois to come to Kansas.

Like most pioneer families, they had their share of hardships and had to live very frugally in order to maintain their vision of the pioneer life. The older sons were able to get work with the railroad at Dodge City, building fence. This eased the family's financial plight to a certain extent.

Tragedy struck in July, 1885, when twenty-two-year-old Andrew, Jr. died of typhoid fever, a dread disease at that time. Three of the remaining four sons settled permanently in the vicinity of northeast Meade County.

Fremont, the eldest, became an extensive land owner and was one of the first farmers of the area to use power machinery for farming. Charles and Forest farmed nearby and were well-known and highly respected in the county.

Will McCauley spent his childhood with his grandparents, attending school at the joint district school known as Richland, approximately eight miles north and one mile west of Fowler. Years later, his daughter, Helen, attended the same school as did the children of Forest McCauley.

When he was sixteen, Will started out independently , working as a cowboy on some of the large ranches along the Cimarron River in Seward County. Some of the cattle drives were long and wearying—on one occasion he told of being in the saddle all day. That night a storm came up with terrific lightning and thunder and no one dared leave the herd. The cowboys were hard-pressed to stay awake until one of their group told them to rub tobacco

156

juice in their eyes. They tried it and he said he could guarantee it to keep one awake.

The year 1894 brought the C.W. Tullis family to southern Gray County. They settled near the McCauley holdings and became well acquainted. On one of his visits with his grandparents, Will met Jessie Tullis, the eldest daughter. The two were married in February, 1898, by the Rev. Howard Gilchrist, son-in-law of Andrew, Sr.

The young couple's first home was on the banks of Crooked Creek in the Whitman House, an abandoned way-station for drivers fording the creek on the historic Jones and Plummer trail. The old rock crossing was just below the house and was still visible until a few years ago.

Being ambitious and possessed of a true pioneer spirit, Will and Jessie decided to homestead in nearby Gray County. They plowed sod to build their three-room sod "mansion" and even managed to improvise running water inside it, a modern innovation for those times.

In October, 1899, the couple's only child, Helen, was born at home. The maternal grandfather rode his then-famous coyote-hunting horse, "Black," all the way to Meade to bring a doctor.

Within a few years, the little girl was spending a lot of time on horseback, usually riding behind the saddle of one of her parents. One of the incidents she remembers vividly is her dad's cow horse, "Old Deck," pitching just for the fun of it on cool mornings. Young McCauley had to work for his neighbors in order to make a living on the new farm; his transportation was "Old Deck," who landed him on the ground occasionally when he got careless or in too much of a hurry. By sheer good fortune, he was never injured in those falls.

The Will McCauley's built a large frame home on land they bought adjoining the rock crossing on Crooked Creek where they started out. They lived there from 1906 until 1947 when they retired to Meade.

Western Kansas' blizzards are indelibly stamped in the memory of pioneers. One in 1909 was outstanding. The day dawned clear with deep snow on the ground from a previous storm. It was Helen McCauley's habit either to ride or drive a horse to the schoolhouse two and a half miles distant. On this morning everyone but the teacher had arrived. He lived in Dodge City and had gone home for the weekend.

The pupils had waited awhile and decided to go home. All arrived home safely and a few minutes later a terrific north wind struck, blowing snow in clouds. The sky became overcast and the temperature dropped to zero.

Will McCauley had gone to Fowler with team and wagon for a load of coal. His wife and child feared for his safety but were faced with the task of closing the barn door to protect the livestock in his absence. Being a resourceful woman, the mother cautioned her daughter to stay inside until she returned and she left the house with a ball of string which she had tied securely to the porch door. Time passed very slowly but eventually, the mother and daughter heard the neighing of an approaching horse above the storm's roar. A snow-covered man made his way to the door. The husband and father had made it back home!

To do so, he had been forced to abandon his wagon about half-way home, turning one of the horses loose and riding the other. Both horses managed to find their way in the blinding storm a distance of about four miles!

The weather remained bad so school was closed for two months, resuming in the spring.

Will and Jessie McCauley at that time farmed parts of three quarters of land. It was a familiar sight to see both in the fields with either a four or six-horse team. The fall of 1912 brought disaster to them and many of their neighbors—an epidemic of sickness killed all but one of their work horses. At that time there was no prevention or cure for the disease.

In a few years, tractors and better machinery made life on the farm much easier. Even after moving to Meade in 1947, the McCauley's spent much time at the farm during planting and harvesting season.

After his wife's death in 1958, Will McCauley live alone in his home in Meade until the last two months of his life, when he moved to the home of his daughter and son-in-law, Mr. and Mrs. William Merkle. His grandchildren and great-granchildren were his chief interest until death came, December 26,1962.

He was the last to bear the McCauley name in or around Meade County, as Forest McCauley and his sons had moved to California in the late 1930's.

Re-printed from" Pioneer Stories of Meade County," 4th Edition; compiled by Meade County Historical Society, Meade County, Kansas, 1985.

PAGE OF THE PAST IS CHISELED IN STONE

A Memorial Day visitor to a little country cemetery is prompted to pause and reflect momentarily on the history of early Meade County that lies at his feet.

One tiny grave is marked with a sleeping lamb carved atop a pillar of white marble. The inscription reads: *"Baby Leon Stockwell, died Dec.23, 1884, age 4 months."*

Nearby a small marker of light grey marble reads: *"Geo. F. Butt, infant, born Sept. 1,1885—Died July 3, 1886."*

Another white marble slab reads simply: *"Lieut.F.E. Hyde, Co.1, 32nd Ohio Infantry."*

Near this can be read: *"Volney Gardner, Dec. 5, 1864—May 31,1885."*

There is the marker bearing the name of Howard H. Gilchrist, 1852—1906. Because of this man's leadership, the cemetery was first begun. The Rev. Gilchrist, Congregationalist minister from Illinois, came west with his family in the late 1870's, accompanying a group of hardy, rugged individuals who were seeking new frontiers to settle. Unlike the "new frontiersmen" of a later day, these men did not believe in the creed of giving "to each accoding to his need, from each according to his ability," but rather they believed the biblical creed, "As a man soweth, that also shall he reap." And they lived accordingly!

Choosing the fertile banks of Crooked Creek approximately six miles north of what is now Fowler, Kansas, these men founded the First Congregational Church of Crook Creek in the year 1879 on land purchased from the late George Emerson of Clark County. Signatures on the original deed, now yellow and brittle with age, show the trustees of the property to have been Silas E. Ayers, W. D. Ayers and H. M. Forbes. The latter was the step-father of the late W. E. McCauley who died at Meade, December 26, 1962.

One of Meade's senior citizens, George Foster, recalls that a member of the McCauley clan invited his family to attend the Sunday service at the little church soon after the Fosters arrived in 1884. He remembers vividly his first visit to the church, how he was greeted by Will McCauley, nine years old at the time and very delighted to see another child at church; he was the first child Mr. Foster had seen here at that time with the exception of members of his own family. The two boys, near the same age, enjoyed each other's company greatly after that and looked forward eagerly to Sunday mornings when they could run and play while their elders visited after services.

Circumstances of that period made it only natural that a cemetery should become a part of the churchyard. It is quite likely that there were burials there prior 1884, but the Stockwell infant's marker is the earliest that remains intact and legible.

One marker attests to the demise of D.C. Rynerson on April 28, 1894. He was the grandfather of Mrs. Eva Clark Nuss of Fowler.

Nearby is the large granite stone bearing the name of Elijah Hutchinson, son of Lewis and Nancy Hutchinson, Born Lincoln County, Kentucky, Jan 24, 1819—died Oct 23, 1887. He was the grandfather of Clarence and Carl Haywood, both of Fowler.

Quite a few markers bear the name, McCauley, as many of that family who came west in 1879 liked Meade County so well that their search for new land ended here. The late Will McCauley was four years old when he made the trip with his grandfather Andrew J.McCauley, Sr., father-in-law to the Rev. Mr. Gilchrist.

The latest burial in the little plot is evidenced by the marker of William Jobling, 1864—1944, beside that of his parents, John and Eliza J. Jobling.

The native wheat grass grows thick and tall over the graves, giving way occasionally to a wild flower in bloom. One must walk carefully in the dense, uneven turf; and, standing there, listening to the wind whip the few remaining trees, one realizes that here, truly, is a page of the past, chiseled in stone.

Ellen Boyd, grand-daughter of Will McCauley

Re-printed from Pioneer Stories of Meade County, 4th edition, Meade County Historical Society, Meade County, Kansas, 1985.

THE MERKLE FAMILY

From Pioneer Stories of Meade County, 4th Edition, 1985.

Written by Howard E. Weller, a son-in-law of Kit and Billie Merkle

In considering the lives of the pioneers it is usually best not to lump them all together for they were individuals, just as we are; and each individual had certain characteristics that made him tick. It was also these characteristics that made him interesting. One person carves a niche for himself where another leaves all and goes "back to the wife's folks." Jesus spoke with his usual wisdom when He said, "No man, having put his hand to the plow, and looking back, is fit for the Kingdom of God." *(Luke 9:26)* The spirit of our hardy pioneers proves this to be true in the worldly sense also.

William(Billie) Merkle and his wife, Catherine, (Kit) early pioneers of Meade County, were a very interesting couple.Billie came to Meade County in the fall of 1884, walking down from Dodge City. He slept out on the prairie alone on his way to a location in Section 2-30-28. We are not told how he was

162

able to locate that particular land but certainly he must have left much behind that one might have looked back at.

Billie was born in Germany and at the age of 14, he came to America because he didn't want to be inducted into the German Army. The first nine years in America he spent with relatives in Virginia, Illinois and Peabody, Kansas, coming to Meade County at the age of 23. There was the business of filing on a homestead and tree claim and making for provision to get through the first winter to be taken care of. Mr. Merkle was aided at this critical time when he obtained work from John Conrad, who lived a few miles down Crooked Creek. In the spring, 10 acres of trees had to be planted on the tree claim. Livestock needed to be acquired to graze the lush virgin plain. Billie bought six head of cows and a buill. In a short while the bull stepped into a prairie dog hole and broke his leg. Sod must be broken out and some kind of crop planted. Billlie obtained a team of oxen with which he attempted to break sod. This proved not so good as these oxen would go only about four and a half rounds in a day. "And when they got that far, even if you were at the far end of the field, you might as well unhitch and go home." The consensus is that the oxen didn't stay long.

Taxes had to be paid in those days as well as no. Billie related that he owed $2.50 in taxes and the sheriff came out after it. "If I hadn't been working for Conrad, I couldn't have paid it," he said.

One of his first horses was "Charlie." Old Charlie, being a pioneer himself was quite a character and no small part of the success of this establishment. These were the days when very few fences were around. Cattle had to be herded. Many were the times that old Charlie was un-hitched from the sod plow and ridden out to turn the cattle while his mate Nancy remained tied to the plow for a rest. When you were out in the field and cattle had to be turned, you didn't bother with the saddle even if you had one. Now old Charlie was built along spare lines and it took some ruggedness to ride him bareback. Mr. Conrad once remarked, "I used to tell Billie his stern end was calloused." About nine years Mr. Merkle went it alone while building his nest. Many problems to solve, many difficulties to overcome but there is no record that he ever looked back. Now if you were up before daybreak and out to the field till noon, how would you get your beans cooked for dinner? According to Billie, you put them on to cook as soon as you got up and let them cook while you feed and harness your horses and mild the cow and eat breakfast. Then the last thing before going to the field you put more buffalo chips in the stove and hopfully go to the field. If the fire last long enough, fine. If too long, well brown beans are good. If not long enough, have something to put your teeth into.

Billie called his half-dugout soddy "Bachelor Hill." Very primitive indeed but sufficient for the time for a man who had his eyes on far horizons. Once a couple of strangers from the east came by nd spent the night with him ; a violent thunderstorm came up. The roof started leaking and one of the visitor jumped up and said, "Come on boys, let's get out of here. She's caving in on us." This was amusing to the rugged pioneer who could make do with almost nothing. During the nine years of bachelorhood the one room soddy was exchanged for a three room "mansion" to which he brought his bride on January 9, 1894.

When you are a bachelor living way out on the prairie, how do you find your mate? Do you just go about your business and one day you look up and there she is?

Well, we have no record of the courtship of Billie Merkle. Suffice to say that it was a great success. When Catherine R. Wolfley came to be the wife of Billie, when was peculiarly fitted to fill the role of companion to a pioneer ranchman. She was mature in years, being 26 at the time, and was also mature in personality, being the fourth child of a family of 13 children. Reared to maturity in Nemaha County in northeast Kansas close to the Potawatomi Indian Reservation, in the adjoining county of Jackson, Kit Wolfley had many times been faced with responsibilities. Once where the younger children were left in her care, she found it necessary to give her brother Jake a whipping. At this time she was quite a good-sized girl. Her mother, on her return, took a dim view of her chastising little Jake and said, "Kit, I'm going to lick you for that!" To which Kit answered, "If you'll lick Jake too, I'll take it; if you won't lick him, I won't." Mrs. Wolfely dropped the matter.

Kit told of a time when her father, treasurer of the school board, had to send her to a board meeting with the books. The clerk of the board sent his books by his son. These two were the only ones at the meeting. Any decisions of lack of decisions had to be made by them!

Kit was also a good student as well as a good speller. She had the habit of winning the spelling bees that were a popular feature of those days. Once when she was unable to attend a spelling bee, it was still reported in the local paper that "The spelling bee last Friday was won by Miss Kitty Wolfley."

Their meeting might never have taken place if her father, Augustus J. Wolfley, hadn't decided to come west for his health. He drove out in a covered wagon. A son, Theodore was already here. Eventually the whole family came out. Their country location was about two miles down Crook Creek from Mr. Merkle'' headquarters. Mrs. Wolfley and the girls lived in Fowler some of the time on account of school. One day, Billie rode by the Wolfley place and stopped for awhile. One of the Wolfley boys, really a young man at the time, had seriously rent his trousers. He had hung a feed sack inside to cover up. As they talked, Billy's horse, Charlie, became interest in the feed sack and managed to get hold of it and out it came. The result was embarrassing exposure. If this happening had any influence in bringing these two families together, it was certainly a fortuitous circumstance of Kit and Billie. When Billie finally brought Kit to the three room mansion, she took her place by his side and never failed in her loyalty and love till death parted them nearly 45 years later. No less loyal and true was he to her. This man and woman were complimentary to each other as is so often the case when two people go through the mill together. Their first child, Matilda, was born here. As time went by and they began to overcome their difficulties, they moved about one mile to a point on Crooked Creek where William J. Merkle was born and now lives. Their other five children were born and grew to maturity here. Industry and frugality were the order of the day in this household. When the family graduated from the sod house, they moved into a frame house composed of two sections which had been moved down from the old Montezuma. Also a large store building from Montezuma was converted into a barn and is still in fairly good repair. Many railroad ties were bought for fence posts from the old Montezuma railroad. These ties were of excellent quality white pine and lasted for many years. Mr. Merkle was an excellent judge of values and never hesitated to take advantage of values he considered good.

After Old Charlie, other horses were added until the breeding of horses and mules became quite a business. At one time, as many as 40 horses and mules were owned. Mostly these were raised to three year olds, then broke to work and sold a few years later. However, some became an integral part of the ranch. Mr. Merkle acquired a sorrel hose called "Slocum" that had taken part in the opening of the Cherokee Strip. Most of the Merkle children learned to ride on Charlie and Slocum.

There was also "Fannie" a gray Percheron brood mare that became the mother of many good horses. Old Fan was always allowed special privileges, so much so that the boys complained about it. Mr. Merkle always said, "You let old Fan alone; she is a very valuable mare." Then the boys took to calling her "Old Valuable."At this stage of development of Western Kansas, all horses were really valuable. People were often judged by the way they treated their horses.

The Merkle's were among the first growers of alfalfa in Meade County. They had many fields up and down the creek. The youngsters found this a little trying. Life just seemed a continual round of stacking hay, going from one field to another and back around again all summer. The Merkle's never let difficulties stop them. They had the philosophy that many of the things that are grievous are good for us. The Merkle alfalfa also contributed to the economy of the community by furnishing labor for some of the neighbors.

Billie Merkle was rugged and energetic. It was sometimes said that he went about his work like killing snakes. At one time, when he had some corn to cut by hand, he hired the late Frank Small to help him.

Frank said that when they went to work, Billie took out through the field like "a house afire." Frank was a large husky man but inexperienced at cutting corn. He said "I couldn't keep in sight of him. When noon time came, I told him I was quitting." Billie asked, "Why? What's the matter?" Frank told him, "I can't keep up." Billie said, "I don't expect you to. Just do what you can."

Kit Merkle had a comforting presence in a sick room and in times of sorrow. Her husband was always willing to share her for such acts of mercy. The Merkles never shirked the hardest tasks but did the things that needed to be done. They gave of themselves when they had nothing else to give and then continued it in later years and better circumstances.

It is good for us to look back on our immediate pioneers and place them in perspective. It is also good for us to voice our appreciation of what they have done for us. Our way has been smoothed and straightened. Let us do what we can to keep it straight. *(Howard Weller, Merkle son-in-law.)*

COUSIN LOYDE SPIVEY'S VIEW

*Reprinted from **Son of the South Wind, My Life in Kansas***

By Loyde Spivey

The dust storm of Palm Sunday, April, 1935

In April, 1935, we had the worst dust storm ever. Fields blew and farm machinery was buried in dirt drifts. Weeds lodged in barbed wire fences and dirt blew into them and only the tops of posts stuck up above the dirt drifts. Cattle walked over fences and wandered. The day the big one came, my parents and we were at my Uncle Walter Tullis' place, where my Granddad Tullis had ranched. It was Sunday at 4 p.m. A real nice sunny day. We were playing cards and visiting. Suddenly it got dark and windy. A huge rolling wave of dirt came over us from the west. Aunt Pearl quickly lit a lamp and soon the air was so full of dirt in the house you could not see the lighted lamp across the room.

About 15 minutes later it got so we could see the yard fence. Mom, Peg and Barbara, age one, stayed there and Dad and I started the 1 ½ mile trip home. We went through the pasture on the way home and tried to drive the milk cows home. The cows would not take a step even when Dad got out of the car and hit them with his hand. The wind was still full of dirt. One could see only a few feet. The air was full of static electricity. The car died as we left Uncle Walter's place. Dirt clogged the air intake on the car and it died. Dad cleaned the intake and tied a red handkerchief on it to stop the dirt and it ran okay for a little way, then died again. We tied one of the old mud chains to the bumper of the car and let it drag on the ground. Then the car ran okay. The chain grounded the static electricity.

However, the cows were another story. The moisture in their eyes caught the dirt until they were blinded by balls of mud over their eyes. Their noses were in bad shape too. When Dad knocked the mud balls from their eyes, they were on their way home. Chickens thought it was night and sat on the ground wherever they were when the storm hit. We did what chores we had to and returned to Walter's. The wind went down some and we all went home.

During the dusty days of 1935, the summer heat was real bad. We moved our bed out into the yard and my folks did too. We covered Barbara's crib with wet sheets to keep the dust out. One night the wind was blowing hard and at midnight the heat stood at 100 degrees. We slept outside several nights.

Loyde's account of his first job at the Fowler Equity Exchange, a farm Co-operative. [Ibid.]

My work at the Co-op was to wait on customers who wanted farm gas tanks filled. The tanks were on trailers they pulled with trucks or pickups. I also screened coal in the winter on snowy days. There was a row of coal sheds and I had to scoop coal over a screen and the fine coal, called slack, was put into burlap sacks. It sold at 35 cents per hundred-weight. We paid $4 per month at the first house (cousin Helen's) when I was getting $65 per month. We paid $7 at the second place. The Co-op had and old ronclad elevator where there was a feed mill grinder, etc., to make poultry and cattle feed. This was in a large warehouse. Also there was an office with a high desk and stove and a little storeroom. I was sent to work there and was soon operating all of the feed business. It was 6:30 a.m. to 6 p.m. The summer was not a real busy time for me as farmers were busy with harvest and field work.

Loyde Spivey worked his way through Kansas Cooperatives and eventually became a manager of grain merchandising operations. The following is taken from the Hutchinson News, Nov.30/1977.

Far-Mar-Co's Loyde Spivey recalls development of co-op grain marketing..
Stories and Photos by Alan Krob, Grain Marketing Editor.

Loyde Spivey, after more than 41 years in cooperatives, walked through the Far-Mar-Co halls for the last time as vice-president of grain operations at 5 p.m. Wednesday, Nov. 30.

Spivey is one of those who came up through the ranks of the cooperative system. His entire career has pivoted around cooperatives—all the way to his retirement. In 1936 he began his co-op career working in a country elevator pit at Fowler, Kan. Spivey served as head of the Farmers Commission

Co's grain sales several years prior to FCC's merger with three other regional grain marketing coops to form Far-Mar-Co in 1968.

Spivey was a farm boy. He says he learned about cooperatives from his father and that knowledge precluded any consideration on his part toward pursuing other career opportunities.

Spivey is a man with strong convictions. "A farmer who owns his farm and machinery and granery has the right to have a jointly-held granery downtown and hire a man to operate it and provide the supplies that he and his neighbors need in the execution of their business," Spivey stated. "The farmer is actually extending himself off the farm through his local cooperative. That's the way it was intended from the beginning of cooperatives and that's the way it is today."

On the regional level, Spivey said he has seen vast improvements in accounting procedures. "These improvements had to come with the volumes of grain we handle on the regional level."

"And then there are the tremendous jobs being done by our transportation departments. With all of the freight rates, transit provisions, Gulf rates, multi-car rates, etc., transportation has become a complex field. It's a science that the regional cooperative has not only had to comprehend, but also know how to operate within its perimeters."

Obviously exports have played an ever-increasing part in the business of the regional cooperative. "Nearly 30 years ago, we were jst beginning to hear the word, 'export' in the trade. We didn't even know how to establish a Gulf bid!" Spivey said. "We've learned!"

On the farm, Spivey said production methods have improved almost beyond comprehension. "The improved farming techniques and the varietal improvements have yielded crops the likes of which none of us would have

170

imagined. Exporting is the answer today with this increased production. I'm firmly convinced of that," Spivey said. "Without exporting, what would we do with all of the excess we're producing?"

Speaking of Promark and his involvement, Spivey said "It's a long-range program. It takes time to develop a system and get it operating smoothly. If producers continue to place a portion of their grain in the program so it can grow and improve, it should become a really important marketing tool for them. It does allow the farmer to participate in long-range world-wide exporting of grain as well as being a factor in long-range planning with domestic users."

In reference to his own career, Spivey said he has many good feelings about it. "The work has been better to me than I could have ever expected. The cooperative system allows one to expand into many fields of work. Mine ran toward marketing of the farmers' grain. It was extremely exciting and enjoyable.

"I tell you now, there was nothing I did on my own that brought me this far, professionally. The credit goes to the people I worked for and with... I've always been able to get up in the morning and look forward to coming to work. It wouldn't be any good if I had to dread coming to a job day after day."

Referring to his early career (of $65 per month and 12 hour days) Spivey said, "That was good money. We had plenty to eat and were comfortable. It was adequate. We were happy then and we are happy now. Cooperatives are a good way of life." *(Hutchinson News, November 30, 1977.)*

* * *

Loyde's parents, Paskel and Grace (Tullis) met at a dance at the Conrad ranch in 1910 or 1911. They were married in a snowstorm in December, 1911, at Meade, Kansas, and went to the Bunyan Hotel in Fowler for their wedding night. They farmed one year near Eva and Elkhart, Kansas. They returned to the Tullis ranch in time for the birth of their one and only child, Loyde, on December 10, 1912.

Paskel died April 8, 1975, and Grace followed on December 5, 1978.

Below:How Uncle Paskel came to be in the Meade-Gray County area.

Paskel was born near Ozark, Missouri, to Will and Candy Spivey, the youngest of eight children. His father was a lay preacher on the street corners in the town.

Red-headed, freckle-faced Paskel went to school, off and on, through the third grade. He turned to working with horses and building railroads by age 12, leaving home by age 16. He worked a few years as a cowboy on the Bevering cattle ranch near Charlie, Texas. Later he traveled by train selling carloads of apples in small towns for a businessman. He sold apples in Fowler, Kansas, and later returned there to work on the Conrad ranch eight miles north and six miles west of Fowler. Shortly after that, he met Grace Tullis.

(Copied from *Son of the South Wind, My life in Kansas, by Loyde Spivey*)

From The Fowler Hustler, Sept. 26, 1906, concerning Hotel Bunyan:

W. P. Bunyan has finished the new Hotel and it is one of the finest ever seen in the West. There is nothing the most exacting or fastidious mind can call for but what it is there. A visit to the great structure will convenience and please anyone. For comfort, convenience, style and appearance, it just can't be excelled anywhere. The new carpets, stylish furniture, artistic painting, decorations and electric lights just caps the climax. Steam heat throughout, cold and hot baths, and everything that mind could think of or money buy is amply provided. This magnificent Hotel will be thrown open to the public in Fowler, Kansas at 8 p.m. On the 4th of October, 1906. Commercial men and tourists in and around Fowler and surrounding towns are invited to come over and spend Sundays where they can have all the comforts and style that the heart could wish. The best of all is that the thousands and thousands of dollars spent in building this modern palace was made by the owner out of the ground right here at Fowler!

HOW PETS ENRICH OUR LIVES

I know I have been criticized by some of my friends for setting such great store by my pets. Surely I was wasting a lot of my time and attention on something that didn't matter. Well, I never thought my pets did not matter. They enriched my life so much that I wanted my children to have the benefit of pets too.

I had some bad spills from horses but was always able to get back up and remount and go on! Sometimes I was hurt a little more than I wanted anyone to know. But I didn't show it. I learned that early on from my parents. Keep your feelings to yourself and keep on keeping on. So that was what I learned to do.

When I lived in Fowler, I had a Belgian Shepherd dog that was my constant companion. He definitely considered himself *my dog* and considered me his mistress. We were inseparable. One day, King was with me out at a chicken coop where I had caught a chicken and was going to have it for supper that night. Without any warning, the dog snarled and lunged for my throat. I put my arm up and his teeth tore into my arm. Fortunately for me, Ivan Masters was working nearby building our garage and heard my scream. By the time he got close enough to throw his hammer at the dog, I had tried to jump over the fence and King had sunk his teeth into my thigh. I was five months pregnant at the time, so wasn't as agile as I might have been otherwise. Ivan's hammer missed hitting the dog but did scare him and he took off in the direction of Dr. Robb's pasture that lay west of our house on the west edge of Fowler. Ivan got me to the house and phoned for help. Frank and the men from the garage came to look for the dog and Dr. Robb came to attend to my wounds. I felt pretty lucky that King hadn't got my throat since that was apparently his target.

Some other men heard of the hunt for the dog and came to help. He was finally shot so that his brain could be sent to Topeka to determine if he was rabid. Meanwhile, Dr. Robb thought I should have the anti-rabies shots and not wait to hear from the State Laboratory. I took the whole series of shots and found them to be not nearly as painful as everyone had said they would be. King turned out not to have rabies. It was postulated at the time that he had just gone "crazy" because he was from a line of very closely inbred Belgian shepherds. I was pretty sure he was "crazy" because I got a look into his eyes at the time he lunged at me. He clearly did not know me at that moment. He looked wild and crazy in his eyes. I was almost heartbroken at losing him but had no choice.

The other dog that I was absolutely crazy about was Capper, an English shepherd. My dad had taken him to get the milk cows in the pasture and he learned to do it all by himself. Every afternoon at four, Capper would head for the pasture without being told. It was as if he had a clock in his head. Always he went out at straight-up four.

One day, unbeknownst to him, the cows had been bothered by heel flies and had come to the shed, hiding back inside where the darkness helped them keep off the flies. Capper went out at four and searched the pasture over thoroughly. Not finding the cows, he came back to the barn only to discover all the cows inside the shed! Always afterward, Capper would go first to the shed and look inside before going out to bring in the cows. It was as if he didn't want that embarrassment again.

My cleanest pet was a pet pig. I wasn't very old—ten maybe, when I raised a baby piglet by hand. She was so smart and so clean. Her conduct certainly belied the expression "filthy as a pig." She had no intention to be filthy about anything and disdained any kind of dirt.

She was also a fastidious eater and never "gobbled" her food "like a hog" but ate very daintily. She was the easiest to "housebreak" of any pet. We were so fond of each other that we were "inseparable" and played for hours at a time. I used to dress her in hand-me-down clothing and pretend that she was another person. The trouble with having a pet like a pig is that there can never be a good outcome. Sooner or later, you have to get rid of it.

That happened to me with several baby calves. They were such babied creatures that they didn't realize they weren't people. They always grew up to be very demanding adults. One baby that I called "Princess" was a fawn colored calf, probably Jersey by breed. She became the most spoiled cow in the county and would stand out at the coral gate telling me how neglected she felt! It is heart-breaking when one finally has to get rid of a pet like that. I shed many a tear over my pets! Then I watched my children do the same thing. I resolved never to deprive my children of pets as long as they would take care of them. Children learn many lessons from their pets, I think.

LESSONS LEARNED ALONG THE WAY

One thing I believe I learned is that every generation wants to make its own mistakes! In spite of all the "pearls of wisdom" we think we have found and polished for our children, they seem to prefer to learn their own lessons—no matter how harsh the teacher. Maybe that is the best way. It is certainly the most painful path.

Being an avid reader all my life, I loved poetry especially and memorized many poems. One that always intrigued me, even to the point that I had it on a plaque on my wall, was *"The House by the Side of the Road."* by Samuel Walter Foss. It's a long poem and I only remember a few lines: ***"Let me live in the house by the side of the road where the race of men goes by; the men who are good and the men who are bad—as good and as bad as I; I would not sit in the scorner's seat nor hurl the cynic's ban; Let me live in the house by the side of the road And be a friend to man."*** Over time, that became my philosophy. I found out it's best not to judge another if you've never walked in his boots. It's easy to judge in our youth. In old age, I see the biblical admonition *"Judge not, lest ye be judged,"* has so much wisdom!

Bibliography
(Published documents.)

Chrisman, Harry E.; Lost Trails of the Cimarron, Denver, CO. 1961.
Martin, Eunice Gilchrist; As I Remember It, Beaverton, OR. 1991
McCauley, Nathan; The McCauley Manifest, Vacaville, CA., 2008.
Spivey, Loyde; Son of the Southwind, My Life in Kansas, Hutchinson,KS, 1998.
Haywood, Robert; On My Father's Side, Topeka, KS., 1975.
Pioneer Stories of Meade County, 4th Ed.,Meade Co. Historical Soc. Meade,KS 1985.
The Fowler News, Fowler, KS.., Jan. 15.,1933.
The Fowler News, Fowler, KS.., Nov. 25, 1937.
The Fowler News, Fowler, KS., Feb. 8, 1940.
Meade Globe-News, Meade, KS., Mar. 28, 1958.
Meade Globe-News, Meade,KS., Dec. 29, 1963.
Dodge City Daily Globe, Dec. 2, 1918.
The Fowler News, Fowler, KS., Nov. 20, 1928.
Young,Frederic; Dodge City, Dodge City,KS., 1972.
Muzzy, David S.; A History of Our Country, Ginn and Company, 1946.

(Unpublished documents.)

Aunt Edna's Journal, a hand-written account of the journey from Iowa to Hamilton
County, Kansas.
Letters from family members and friends.

Errata: p.69,lines 2-5,from Robert Haywood,
On My Father's Side, 1975,as he defined "The
Protestant Ethic" from Calvin's theology.Also
p.138,line 4, "Their daughter" should read
"Carl's sister." In spite of best effort , errors
include family tree branches and varying dates.